"Noah Sanders has written a groundbreaking book. I say Noah's book is groundbreaking because it is the first and only book I've ever read that looks at farming and agriculture from God's point of view, as revealed in Scripture. Every Christian who either grows (or has a hankering to grow) a garden, or desires to be any sort of larger-scale farmer, needs to read *Born-Again Dirt*. It is a biblical-agrarian primer, laying a proper foundational understanding for God-honoring agriculture. Noah is a young man but he has written a book that is full of old and largely forgotten (or totally ignored) wisdom. It is abundantly clear in reading *Born-Again Dirt* that Noah is an intelligent, clear-thinking, humble, and biblically-grounded person. I dare say his thoughts and conclusions are inspired. *Born-Again Dirt* is destined to become a classic in the world of contra-industrial, Christian-agrarian literature. It is the kind of book that, when read, understood, and applied by young Christians today, will lead to proper perspectives and proper understandings and proper actions. And, years from now, those people will look back and realize how influential the book was in their lives. I believe that agriculture is a high and holy calling for God's people, and *Born-Again Dirt* is an excellent guide for Christians who feel that calling."

—*Herrick Kimball, author of* The Deliberate Agrarian *blog*

"This young man is a breath of fresh air! I don't know of another book on farming/gardening that has both practical, how-to information and shows us that God cares about our hearts as we farm."

—*Susan Vinskofski, author of the blog learningandyearning.com*

"[A] very good book and one I think that should be read by all. Not that everyone will be looking to farm[,] but . . . Noah does a good job of showing how to take ones vocation and apply God's word to it."

—*Tony Konvalin, homesteader and blogger*

"[I]f you are wanting a big picture visionary book you will love this one. You might also fall under conviction reading as I did."

—*Steve Donahue at www.thelegacypodcast.com*

BORN-AGAIN DIRT

BORN-AGAIN DIRT
FARMING TO THE GLORY OF GOD

Cultivating a Biblical Vision for God-Glorifying Agriculture

NOAH SANDERS

foreword by JOEL SALATIN

Born-Again Dirt by Noah Sanders
© 2013 Noah Sanders
All Rights Reserved.

Published by Rora Valley Publishing
www.roravalleypublishing.com

ISBN: 978-0-9851315-4-8

First Edition, January 2012
Second Edition (various grammatical corrections, added foreword, added appendix), May 2013

Front cover and author photographs: Abigail Sanders
Back cover photograph: Joel Ferrill
Editors and Proofreaders: Lora Lynn Fanning, Timothy Sanders, Noah Sanders, Kyle
    Shepherd, Jack and Marilou Dody
Illustrations: Noah Sanders
Typesetting and interior layout: Kyle Shepherd
Cover design: Kyle Shepherd

DEDICATION

To my son, Enoch Timothy Sanders.

I pray that the Lord will draw you to Himself
so you can be born again at a young age.
May He bless you and bring glory to Himself
through the work and testimony of your life.

TABLE OF CONTENTS

APPENDIX C

APPENDIX D

FOREWORD

by Joel Salatin

GROWING UP IN A CONSERVATIVE CHRISTIAN HOME ON OUR BEYOND organic family farm in the 1960s, I lived in two different worlds. Our church friends lived in one world, but our family farm lived in another. My Dad and Mom, ultra conservative by any standard, routinely befriended hippies and our house often had dope-smoking mother-earthers hanging around talking about compost, dome homes, and Viet Nam war atrocities.

On Sunday, of course, I spent the day with straight-laced Bible fundamentalists who made jokes about hippies and those mother earthers. When Dad made Adelle Davis' Tiger Milk, a concoction of brewer's yeast, honey, raw milk from our Guernsey cows, and I can't remember what else, our church buddies called it Panther Puke. I grew up on Bible memory programs and *Mother Earth News* magazine.

While our church friends made jokes about environmentalists, in our house *The Whole Earth Catalogue* stimulated many great discussions. Our family routinely patronized the health food store when it first came to town, a place our Christian friends thought cultish. How could a Christian patronize a place that smelled like incense, sold tofu, and had Zen literature stashed about? Our Christian friends built Tyson chicken houses and confinement dairies, used pharmaceuticals indiscriminately and poured on chemical fertilizer. Even their backyard gardens received liberal (a judicious use of the word liberal, to be sure) doses of insecticide just to be safe.

The whole notion that farming and food systems could contain a moral implication couldn't make it past the laughter and jokes about environmentalist pinko commies. Yet our family plugged on, eschewing chemicals, building compost piles, planting trees, and attending environmental farming conferences. As our farm began attracting attention, most visitors were tree-hugging cosmic nirvana creation-worshippers. We used these visits to plant seeds of Biblically-based stewardship as Creator-worshippers. That sure made for some interesting conversations.

Over the years, I've seen an amazing transformation in our farm visitors. Today, probably half are conservative home-schooling Christians. I believe that the home-schooling movement spawned an entire awakening to alternative ideas. Families who left the conventional institutional educational setting, who disagreed with credentialed officialdom, found their new path soul satisfying. That satisfaction led them to ask the question: "Well, I wonder what else I've been missing out on?"

This quest for a narrow way within a broad way cultural context led families to chiropractors (what, those quacks?), nutrition, cottage-based businesses and home-based self-reliance. The home school idea literally sprouted kitchen sprout growing, raw milk consumption, gardens, and domestic flour mills for home-baked breads.

I believe the Christian community, which should have been the repository of "fearfully and wonderfully made," squandered this high moral ground of environmental stewardship. Today, young people like Noah Sanders are beginning to chip away at the stereotype of the creation-exploitive (just one notch below rapist) religious right. When members of the religious right espouse creation stewardship, people listen to the Biblical redemption message who would never give it a thought otherwise.

In this great introductory and thought-provoking book, Noah Sanders dares to invoke a moral dimension into vocational farming. I am thrilled to see young people like him grasp this cornerstone of Christian credibility. Bringing every life dimension captive to God's mind has far-reaching implications in our day-to-day decisions. Thank you, Noah, for broaching this subject in this context. It's sorely needed and should stimulate both personal soul-searching and healthy corporate discussions.

ACKNOWLEDGMENTS

I WANT TO THANK THE MANY PEOPLE THAT WORKED TO MAKE THIS book possible.

First, my wife DOROTHY—you are the joy of my life, and such an encouragement. I am so blessed to be married to such a godly woman. Your passion for the Lord and for growing things has helped strengthen mine. Without your support and love this book wouldn't exist.

My parents, TIM AND WENDI SANDERS—you have been the most influential people in my life. Thank you for being willing to be different in the way you raised me in order to prepare me to be a man of God. Your wisdom, counsel, and support have been the key the Lord has used in the success He has given me. Thanks for all the late night talks, help with projects, and being willing to listen to all my "ideas" through the years. Thanks for all your help with this book, including the recent sleepless nights editing.

My SIBLINGS—you are a great encouragement to me. Thanks for all your help with the farm and other projects. I don't know any group of people I would rather work with. Thanks, ABBI, for taking the photos for the cover of this book.

My father-in-law, MICHAEL B. MORTON—thanks for lending me Joel Salatin's book *You Can Farm* many years ago. The Lord used it to help start me on the journey of farming. Your enthusiasm and encouragement for this book have meant a lot to me.

KYLE SHEPHERD—for volunteering your design skills and for the wholehearted effort that you put into making this the best possible book you could. It's incredible how the Lord brought you along at just the right time. I'm excited about your vision for producing God-glorifying books and look forward to seeing the ministry God gives you as a result of your faithfulness on this book.

My older sister LORA LYNN—thanks for working on editing my book. Even while pregnant, on bed-rest, and with a houseful of energetic youngsters.

JOEL FERRILL—thanks for helping me keep caught up with farm work while I have worked on this book. Your faithfulness in work and service are an inspiration to me. I look forward to what the Lord is going to do in your life.

JOEL SALATIN and his books—thanks for giving me a vision for applying a Biblical worldview to the way I farm, and providing the advice that has enabled me to farm for a living.

There are countless other people who have contributed to the writing and work of this book. I am sorry I can't mention all of you here. I would have to write another book just to adequately give credit and thanks.

Last, but not least, I want to wholeheartedly give thanks to THE LORD for His mercy and grace. He knows the wickedness of my heart, and still saved me. And He graciously allows me to walk with Him and be a steward of His land. I long for the day that I shall walk with Him in the new land that He is preparing for us.

INTRODUCTION

"So whether you eat or drink, or whatever you do, do it all for the Glory of God." 1 Corinthians 10:31

WHEN I STARTED FARMING SEVERAL YEARS AGO, THIS IS THE BOOK I wanted to read. When the Lord began to convict me that my farm needed to bring glory to Him in the way it was designed and operated, I found there were very few resources to encourage and equip me. The majority of farming books weren't written by authors with a biblical worldview, with the refreshing exception of Joel Salatin. His books were extremely inspiring and instilled in me a desire to explore how my love for the Lord Jesus Christ should affect the way I farmed and viewed farming. Finding no existing books, I ended up doing my own informal research, and eventually felt that the Lord wanted me to write a book for the encouragement of other Christian farmers. After much toil and labor, this is the imperfect result.

The primary message of this book is that the transforming work of the Gospel in the hearts of farmers should also transform our agriculture. If we want to glorify God we must be Christian farmers, not just farmers who are Christians. The way we work the dirt must spring from a Biblical worldview. This is the concept of "born-again dirt".

This book is primarily written for the growing number of Christian families and individuals who are moving back to the land and trying to learn to farm. This includes me. As the Lord works in our lives to change our hearts I believe we begin to value the benefits that an agrarian lifestyle offers:

* The ability to work with our hands

- The opportunity to work with and spend time with family

- The bountiful harvest of healthy, fresh food

- The reliability of providing directly for our needs in a fragile economy

However, there is a danger.

If we don't recognize the spiritual battleground within agriculture and purposely lay a biblical foundation for the way that we farm, then we will fail to give glory to God in our farming. Agriculture is dominated today by those who deny God's existence or ownership of all creation, or by those who live as though He doesn't impact our lives or the way we farm. And they are the ones, unfortunately, who provide the majority of the farming training resources available to us inexperienced Christian back-to-the-landers. We must equip ourselves with a solid, Biblical, agricultural worldview through which we can filter this information, or we will end up worshiping their idols.

I have begun the journey of transforming my farm so that every aspect of it is based in God's Word. This is what I mean by having dirt that is "born-again." Perhaps some people may be uncomfortable with my use of this term, but I believe it helps communicate the fact that Christians must view farming differently than non-Christians. A man who has been born-again has been given a new heart, and this new birth changes his perspective on the entire world. A farmer who is born-again should adopt God's perspective on everything he does, including farming.

I am not a skilled writer, but I would like to share with the body of Christ some of the things I am learning from God that might be of benefit to others. My purpose is not to provide all the answers, but instead to raise questions, look at Scripture, share testimony, and provide practical examples of application. I am not as concerned with convincing you to adopt particular methods as I am with challenging you to adopt biblical thinking as the foundation for your methods.

My desire is to see Christian farmers around the world begin a journey of seeking to glorify God though their farms. I want to see the whole Church rise up and take back agriculture for the Kingdom of God by not only farming, but also by being willing to support Godly farming. I believe this will result in the spread of the Gospel of Christ and also in the most successful farms the world has ever known.

To God be the Glory!

1

BORN-AGAIN DIRT

A vision for Christian agriculture

I HAVE THE INCREDIBLE PRIVILEGE OF BEING A FARMER. NOT MANY people in America can say that any more. In the mid 1800s, 2 out of every 3 men you met were farmers. Today, farmers make up less than .05% of the work force (1 out of 2000). We all know, however, that farming is not some old fashioned occupation that will fade away with the wagon makers and cobblers of yesterday. Production of food is essential to the survival of our economy and there will always be a need for those who work the dirt.

I became interested in farming as a young man after trying to grow some food for my family in our small garden. In previous years the garden had always grown up in weeds when the heat of summer came on, but I was inspired by a gardener friend and tackled the neglected soil. I found that working the soil offers an amazing sense of satisfaction through being able to work hard, care for the plants, and eat the fruits of my labor.

I believe the reason many people gain so much enjoyment from the care of the land is because it's one of the most basic means of fulfilling the job God has given us—to rule His creation. In Genesis, after God created man, He told him be fruitful, multiply, fill the earth, and rule over the rest of creation. He then placed him in a garden and told him to work and care for it (Genesis 2:15). Although farming is not the only way of taking dominion, it seems that farming and agriculture should be one of the normal and foundational occupations of His people, rather than one of the rarest as we see today.

I was primarily attracted to the benefits that a farming lifestyle would have on my life. My desire was to have a job where I could have my own business and work with my family. I explored several other ventures, including blacksmithing (yes, an even more obscure occupation than farming, but still alive nonetheless) and musical instrument repair. But when I considered farming and the lifestyle that it offered I was hooked. Not only did it provide the opportunity to work for myself and include my family in my work, but it also involved interesting and creative work that changes with the seasons. The aspect of being able to grow my own food without being dependent on the grocery store appealed to me. And I liked the fact that I was producing something, food, that met the real needs of people.

Today there seems to be a growing number of other Christians and Christian families who are beginning to recognize the benefits of a farming lifestyle. They are learning to grow gardens, milk a cow, raise chickens, and sell the stuff they grow.

FARMING TO THE GLORY OF GOD

As Christian farmers we should all agree that we desire to glorify God in the way we farm. Most of us are familiar with the following verse:

> So whether you eat or drink, or whatever you do, do it all for the
> glory of God. (1 Corinthians 10:31)

As Christians we love the Lord, and desire to please Him in what we do. But the question is, how do we do that with something like agriculture?

When I first started farming I tended to think that bringing glory to God through farming meant to be the best farmer I could be while conducting myself in a moral way. You know, be honest, don't steal, try to look out for others first, follow the Golden rule, work hard, etc. In a word, try to be a good Christian while trying to be a successful farmer.

So I tried it. I began to read and talk to experts to learn all I could about farming. We lived in a university town with an agricultural school and I had access to lots of resources. I planted a larger garden, acquired some bees, and raised some chickens.

I soon began to notice, however, that not all the experts agreed on how to farm! For instance, some were more industrial and scientific in their approach and others were more environmental and natural. And even within those two approaches there were differences. Farming, I found out, wasn't as black and white as math or physics. If you asked a dozen math teachers what two plus two equals, they would all say four. But if you asked a dozen experienced gardeners how to grow a tomato, you would probably get twelve different answers. So how was I to know which way I should grow a tomato? What I had started out doing was going to the world's experts and using their answers. But even if they had some good ideas, they weren't always right. In fact, many of their methods seemed to be inconsistent with my desire to glorify God in the way I farmed.

THE IMPACT OF WORLDVIEW ON AGRICULTURE

I began to realize that the way someone farms has a lot to do with his beliefs. A person's goals, view of life and its origin, and understanding of right and wrong all impact the way he looks at agriculture. It's not just about deciding which approaches will work, it's about making his practices consistent with his view of the world.

The more I learned the more clearly I began to see the worldviews of different farming experts and how these affected their view of agriculture.

For instance, the most prevalent method of agriculture today, industrial agriculture, seems to be based on a worldview that ignores God and elevates man and his wisdom as the source of truth. This humanistic worldview results in a form of agriculture whose primary objective is maximum yield and profit and whose ultimate source of wisdom is science. Hence the large scale and complex technology of industrial agriculture.

Environmental, organic agriculture, on the other hand, seems to be based on a worldview that worships nature. For them the goal is to preserve and learn from nature, and this results in more natural farm-ing methods.

It became apparent to me that there was more to farming for the glory of God than just being a good, moral farmer. If the beliefs and worldviews of these "experts" impacted the methods that they devel-oped for farming, then shouldn't I be trying to apply a Biblical world-view to the way I farm? Does God care about the design of my farm, or production methods, or what types of crops I grow? Could it be that I need to express my worship of God not only in my conduct, but also in the very decisions I make about how to farm?

In my quest to become a successful farmer for the glory of God I had overlooked the fact that success is a very relative term. It depends on the goals that are used to define success. I had been trying to pursue the world's standards for successful farming. And even they involved a contradiction. If I was a successful industrial farmer, it would make me an unsuccessful organic farmer. And if I was a successful organic farmer, then I would be an unsuccessful industrial farmer. If I wanted to be a farmer that glorified the Lord, I needed to be successful ac-cording to His definition.

Gradually the Lord began to show me that the transformation of my heart should transform the way I farmed. Just putting a Christian fish symbol on my farm truck didn't mean I was bringing glory to God if my farming methods reflected a pagan worldview.

For my farm to bring Him glory, it needed to reflect the fact that it was run by a born-again farmer. My agriculture needed to be built on a biblical foundation. My dirt needed to be "born-again" dirt.

WHAT IS "BORN-AGAIN" DIRT?

"Born-Again Dirt" is *God-glorifying agriculture that springs from a Biblical worldview.*

Sometimes it's helpful to use a new term when we want to gain a new perspective. When I arrived at the realization that God-glorifying agri-culture required a transformation in the foundation and direction of my farm, I wanted a distinctive term to describe it. I believe born-again dirt is a term that can help us think differently about what Christian agriculture should look like. It helps communicate the fact that our dirt (agriculture) needs to be born again (changed as a result of our new hearts).

God calls Christians to be different than the world. When we are born again God gives us new hearts as new creations, and we must not live as we did before. No longer are we a slave to the worldviews of this world. We now have a worldview that is to be based on the Word of God. Everything that we do, including farming, must reflect the new heart and change of values Christ has given us.

In Romans 12:1–2 we read:

> Therefore, I urge you, brothers, in view of God's mercy, to offer your bodies as living sacrifices, holy and pleasing to God—this is your spiritual act of worship. Do not conform any longer to the pattern of this world, but be transformed by the renewing of your mind. Then you will be able to test and approve what God's will is—his good, pleasing and perfect will.

This verse shows us that our worship is not just about changing our schedule on Sunday morning, it involves submitting our whole lives to the will of God. Our worship of God should impact the way that we farm as we submit every part of it to His will. The renewing of a farmer's mind by the Gospel should transform his agriculture so that it no longer conforms to the pattern of this world.

As Christians the goal of anything we do in life should ultimately be the glory of God. That should be the object of our farming. But we don't glorify God in farming through merely saying that's what we want to do. It has to be evidenced in the way we live.

> Let your light so shine before men, that they may see your good works, and glorify your Father which is in heaven. (Matthew 5:16, KJV)

To glorify God our farms should provide a testimony of the good works that God gave us to do. And to do that, our farms must be examples of applying the truths of Scripture.

> All Scripture is God breathed and is useful for teaching, rebuking, correcting and training in righteousness, so that the man of God may be thoroughly equipped for every good work. (1 Timothy 3:16–17)

If we want to be successful Christian farmers who glorify God, then we must have born-again dirt. Dirt that is no longer based on the principles of this world, but upon the principles of God's Word. I am *not* trying to apply the term "born-again" to mean the process of sanctification, but I want to use it to communicate the change that must take place in the approach to farming as a result of a farmer's salvation.

BEGINNING THE JOURNEY

The gradual realization that I needed to have born-again dirt began a journey for me of daring to hold every aspect of my agriculture up to the Word of God. I began looking to the Scriptures to see what God said about farming and agriculture. I examined the different areas of my farm: design, production, management, marketing, etc., to see how I could begin applying God's principles. The more I learned and the more I applied, the more I saw the benefits of farming God's way, and I desired to encourage other Christian farmers to take the same journey.

Born-again dirt is not a *legalistic* approach to farming, but rather an approach based on the *heart*. It's not about trying to come up with the perfect Biblical method of farming and convincing everyone to adopt it. Instead, it's about acknowledging God and seeking to apply and honor His principles in the way we farm.

I believe there are many methods of farming we can develop that are consistent with God's Word. These will depend on your climate, resources, markets, etc. My desire in writing this book isn't to convince you to farm like I do, but to encourage you to begin a journey of reforming your farm to be more conformed to the principles of Christ.

The Christian life is a journey, not an event. In the same way that our lives don't become perfect when we are born again, our farms don't become perfect either. Instead, when we are born again our lives become Christ-centered and He takes us

> *Born-again dirt is not a legalistic* APPROACH *to farming, but rather an approach based on the* HEART.

on a journey of sanctification, exposing and cleansing one sinful area of our lives at a time. Agriculture is one of those areas. As a farmer, I seek to understand why God wants me to farm and how He wants me to farm so that He may be glorified through me.

I invite you to join me in this little book as we consider what born-again dirt could look like. We'll focus on the major points, and there will be many things not covered and many questions not answered. But I pray that the Lord will use the thoughts that are here to encourage you as you seek to have born-again dirt.

2

LAYING A BIBLICAL FOUNDATION

The proper foundation for agriculture

BORN-AGAIN DIRT MUST BE FOUNDED IN THE WORD OF GOD. IN ORDER to glorify God in the way that we farm, it's necessary to have a proper Biblical foundation. Just as the parable of the wise and foolish builders teaches, if we don't build on a foundation of obedience to what God has told us, then what we build will fall. It's also like planting a garden. If your soil isn't good, then nothing you plant will amount to much. In farming, the right foundation and the right soil are based on the Word of God.

There is a danger for many of the new Christian farmers that I see getting started today. They unknowingly adopt worldly methods that don't bring glory to God. When you first start farming and you don't know *anything*, you have to look somewhere for answers. The primary sources of agricultural information available today are from those who reject God or believe He's not relevant to agri-

> *In farming, the right foundation and the right soil are based on the Word of God.*

culture. If we don't make sure that we lay a strong biblical foundation upon which to build our farms, then we will waste a lot of time building something that won't last.

BASIC PRINCIPLES OF A BIBLICAL
WORLDVIEW OF AGRICULTURE

1. WE DON'T OWN OUR FARMS

If we want to have a proper, biblical view of farming, the first thing
we need to recognize is that God is the creator and ruler of all creation.
This means that our lives, our farms, and everything else belongs to
Him. Psalms 24:1 tells us, "The earth is the Lord's, and everything in
it." If we want to honor the Lord through the way we farm, we have to
understand that the dirt we work isn't ours.[1]

If we go out to our farms and say, "What could I get out of this
land?", we are asking the wrong question. We are thinking like the
owner of our farm, rather than the steward of it. *If we treat the land like
it's ours, we are acting like thieves.* Instead, we need to be asking, "What
does the Lord want me to do with the land and resources He has entrusted to me?"

Even though the dirt we work belongs to God, He has made us stewards of it. After creating everything else, God made man and put him
in charge of the earth.

> "Then God said, "Let us make man in our image, in our likeness,
> and let them rule over the fish of the sea and the birds of the air,
> over the livestock, over all the earth, and over all the creatures
> that moves along the ground." (Genesis 1:26)

When God made man in His own image, it was so that man could reflect His glory. And one of the ways I believe God intends for man to do

---

1   We don't own our land . . . but neither does anyone else. God is the ultimate owner of the
land and He delegates stewardship directly to individuals. This means that He also delegates
temporary ownership and rights to those individuals so they can properly fulfill their responsibilities as stewards. God always gives authority along with responsibility. I haven't found any
Scriptures indicating that God delegates general ownership of land to civil governments who
in turn give individuals the privilege of working it. If I am the one who is going to have to
give an account one day for how I care for my land, then I must have the authority to do with
it what I feel God wants. We must realize the importance of strong property rights to good
stewardship and not get caught up in godless, idealistic socialism.

this is by putting the same care and creativity into managing creation as He did in making it.

As stewards we don't have the right to do whatever we want with our farms. We have a responsibility to do what the Owner of our farms wants in the way He wants it done.

When we get to heaven one day and have to give an account of our whole lives, will God look at the way we cared for the farms He gave us and say, "Well done good and faithful servant!"? Or will He say, "Why were you not faithful to care for it in the way I wanted?"

2. FARMING IS NOT ABOUT US

I know it's shocking, but if we want to have born-again dirt, we must realize that farming isn't all about us! Again, we probably all agree with this, but it's easy to become selfish farmers, just like it's easy to become selfish in anything we do. Jesus illustrated this very plainly in the following parable of the foolish farmer.

> "Watch out! Be on your guard against all kinds of greed; a man's life does not consist in the abundance of his possessions."
>
> And he told them this parable: "The ground of a certain rich man produced a good crop. He thought to himself, 'What shall I do? I have no place to store my crops.' Then he said, 'This is what I'll do. I will tear down my barns and build bigger ones, and there I will store all my grain and my goods. And I'll say to myself, "You have plenty of good things laid up for many years. Take life easy; eat, drink and be merry."'
>
> But God said to him, 'You fool! This very night your life will be demanded from you. Then who will get what you have prepared for yourself?' This is how it will be with anyone who stores up things for himself but is not rich toward God." (Luke 12:15–21)

The farmer in the parable was a successful farmer according to today's standard of success. He had grown so much food that he didn't have enough room to store it all. However, he was not successful in God's eyes because he saw his wealth as a way to bring him ease and pleasure.

The goal of farming isn't just to make money off the land. The goal is to love God by reflecting His image as we care for His creation and produce food and fiber that provide for the needs of others.

3. GOD KNOWS MORE ABOUT FARMING THAN WE DO

God is the foremost farming "expert." He is the source of all wisdom. He not only designed and created everything, but He planted the first garden. It makes sense that the best farming is going to be based on God's wisdom, not man's. The infinite knowledge and understanding that backs up God's designs and models makes the knowledge of an agricultural scientist seem insignificant.

Thankfully for us, God has revealed His wisdom to His people though His Word and creation. These are the sources we need to look to when we are trying to learn how to farm.

The Bible is the farmer's sufficient guide to having a proper understanding about what God wants him to do. It's not a step-by-step "how to" manual, but it gives a framework that equips us to know how to answer every question.

> All Scripture is God-breathed and is useful for teaching, rebuking, correcting and training in righteousness, so that the man of God may be thoroughly equipped for every good work. (2 Timothy 3:16–17)

You may be saying, but that verse isn't talking about farming. No, not directly, but I believe that when it talks about "every good work", that includes farming, which was the good work that God gave to Adam before the fall (Genesis 2:15).

Creation is the manifestation of God's character in the work of His hands. When we look at the creation we see the beauty, the power, the wisdom, the creativity, the care, and the love of God clearly reflected. Creation is a vast library of wisdom for the farmer who seeks to care for and work it. From the brilliant design of a leaf with its looping system of distribution to the symbiotic relationship of plants and animals, God's design is a blueprint for how we should farm.

> For since the creation of the world God's invisible qualities—his eternal power and divine nature—have been clearly seen, being

understood from what has been made, so that men are without excuse. (Romans 1:20)

It's so easy to trust in our own experience and intellect to help us figure out the best way to farm. But experiential knowledge must be based in revealed knowledge. This means that when we are listening to the advice of other farmers who have more experience, we need to be filtering everything they are saying through a Biblical worldview. The Lord can then give us wisdom to sift out the beneficial from the junk.

If we as Christians look to God as the foremost farming expert and seek to learn from His Word and creation, then I believe we will become the best farmers in the world.

4. WE CAN'T MAKE THINGS GROW!

> So neither he who plants nor he who waters is anything, but only God, who makes things grow. (1 Corinthians 3:7)

If you are a farmer, then you realize that you aren't in control of everything that affects your farm. Rain, hail, drought, disease, and pests can impact the production and fruitfulness of our farms, and we can't do anything about it most of the time. Even if nothing ever went wrong, we still can't take credit for things going right. We can't make things grow. We can plant seeds and care for animals and water the ground, but unless God causes increase we won't accomplish anything.

As Christian farmers we must recognize that we are *completely* dependent on the Lord to make us succeed. A successful farm comes not from our own strength or skill, but from God blessing our faithfulness.

One of my older Christian neighbors was once approached by an extension agent who asked, "Mr. Hay, I have noticed that every year you have a beautiful garden. What is your secret?" My neighbor replied in his deep, dignified southern accent, "Well, first we work hard to prepare the soil for planting. Then we look in the almanac to see what day would be good for planting according to the moon,

As Christian farmers we must recognize that we are COMPLETELY *dependent on the Lord to make us succeed.*

for the Bible says the moon was created to mark times and seasons. And after we get everything in the ground I go sit on that log over by the side of the garden, take off my hat, and pray, "Lord, we've done the best we know how. Now it's up to you to give us a good garden."

I don't think that extension agent went around telling Mr. Hay's secret to a good garden, but I think Mr. Hay had hit the nail on the head. Our job is to be faithful, and the fruit is up to the Lord.

Many of us farmers struggle with worry. When there are so many things out of our control, we tend to worry about whether all our hard work will pay off in the end. However, Christ commands us not to worry. It's a sin not to trust in the Lord. He provides for the birds and the flowers, and He will provide for us if we are faithful to be obedient to Him. When the Lord does bless us, we need to acknowledge that the increase of the land is a gift of God, not an automatic right that we have because of our work. May we never boast save in the Lord.

> For who makes you different from anyone else? What do you have
> that you did not receive? And if you did receive it, why do you boast
> as though you did not? (1 Corinthians 4:7)

Instead of worrying or being prideful, we as Christian farmers need to be characterized by thankfulness. And not just thankfulness when things seem to be going well, but also when they seem to be falling apart. We know that God is sovereign and in control, and He often uses trials and troubles to build our faith, increase our wisdom, and draw us closer to Him.

> Though the fig tree does not bud, and there are no grapes on the
> vines. Though the olive crop fails and the fields produce no food.
> Though there are no sheep in the pens, and no cattle in the stalls,
> yet I will rejoice in the Lord. I will be joyful in God my Savior.
> (Habakkuk 3:17– 18)

FARMING AND THE GOSPEL

The gospel, the primary message of the Bible, has great impact on farming. Man was given stewardship of the earth at the very beginning of the world. God gave him a mission and everything he needed to carry it out. However, man rebelled against God and the plan He had for him and sin entered the world. Man was then enslaved to sin and could no longer live in a way that pleased the Lord. The ground was cursed and man's job of caring for and working the earth was made much harder. God was merciful, though, and displayed His love by sending His Son, Jesus, to do what we couldn't do: live a perfect life and suffer the punishment for our own sins.

As Christian farmers who have been saved from our sin by the blood of Christ, we should not despair as we labor under the effects of the curse. However, what we can and should do as Christians is seek to apply the redemption of Christ to every area of our lives, including agriculture. We allow the law of Christ to root out wickedness and disobedience and plant seeds of righteousness and obedience. As Christian farmers we must trust that the Lord will enable us by His strength to faithfully work out our mission of stewardship. Unlike other farmers, we have a hope in the fact that Christ is returning to restore all things and that this current world, groaning under the curse of sin, is only temporary.

CONCLUSION

If we want to have born-again dirt, one of the first steps of the journey is developing the proper heart, understanding, or worldview that God wants us to have in regard to working the dirt. This is foundational to building God-glorifying agriculture. In farming, if we want our crops to produce fruit then we need to sow them in the right soil. The same goes with farming in general. If we want our farms to produce the fruit that God desires, then they need to be rooted in the Word of God.

3

EVALUATING OUR AGRICULTURE

Does modern farming reflect a biblical foundation?

In this chapter, I want to examine our need for born-again dirt. I want to take a look at where we are today, and see where we need to be headed. Many people, especially those who don't farm, aren't aware of any real need to improve our agriculture. So it's important that we recognize the error and consequences of ungodly farming. I want to look at some of the problems in agriculture today and evaluate the worldviews of the underlying philosophies. However, the reason for this review isn't to criticize where we are today, but to try to help us see where we need to go from here.

FLAWS PRESENT IN MODERN AGRICULTURE

American agriculture is viewed by many people in the world as the shining example of successful agriculture. With our countless acres of grain in the Midwest, our California valleys bursting with vegetables, our feedlots full of beef and our barns packed with pigs and poultry, we seem to be on the cutting edge of food production. Our methods appear to be beyond question when you compare us with places like Africa, where people are starving amid plentiful resources because of poor farming methods.

The American consumer shows that they trust in the current system of agriculture by risking their survival on the fact that there will be food on the grocery store shelves tomorrow. And it's no wonder, considering the unprecedented reliability with which the shelves are filled year round with an array of cheap, tasty food. Normally only buying what they need for the week, the average person puts their faith in the integrity of American agriculture by never even questioning its ability to provide the food they need. But is this faith well founded, or do we need to reexamine the health and integrity of our systems?

When I first started to pursue being a farmer, I quickly began to discern an unrecognized but fairly obvious fact: behind modern agriculture's smiling, glowing face there are many glaring problems. Some of these problems could potentially lead America into a food crisis and famine in the not too distant future. Other problems are already affecting the health of many Americans today.

UNPROFITABLE FARMING

Government intervention and industrial farming methods have made it very difficult for all but a few American farmers to make a living. When the government subsidies keep unprofitable farmers in business it becomes very difficult for the profitable farmers to compete with them. The best thing the government could do for farming is to let unsuccessful farmers go out of business so they can be replaced with better ones.

Industrial farming is dependent on government subsidies to compensate for artificially low prices of commodities like corn. Government support of industrial farming practices has resulted in the necessity of huge farms and large machinery in order to be somewhat profitable. This scale of production requires a huge investment of capital to get started.

I was talking to a retired extension agent and he said, "If someone wanted to start farming today they would need a million dollars. And if I had a million dollars I wouldn't be a farmer!" A study claimed the fact that the income of the average farming family is now the same as for other occupations. However, the study admitted that eighty-seven percent of their income came from off-farm jobs![1]

No Replacement Farmers

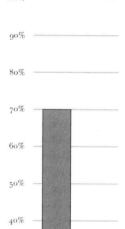

PERCENTAGE OF FARMERS
THEN AND NOW

Few young people are drawn into farming because of the lack of profitability and our culture's disparaging view of hard, manual labor. As a result the current farming population is aging. I mentioned in the first chapter that since 1830 America has gone from around 70% of its workers being farmers to 0.05% in 2008. That's from 2 out of three to 1 in 2000! Very few Americans farmers are young people, with the average age of the farmer being over 55 years old. Of all U.S. farmers only 5.8% were under the age of 35 in 2002.

Unhealthy Food

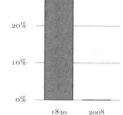

Most American farmers today have little financial incentive to produce healthy food. The wholesale market rewards quantity of production, and only demands that food be "safe." It's not that our agriculture tries to produce bad food. We have entire government agencies that try to prevent dangerous foods from entering the market. But just having food that doesn't make us sick or kill us immediately doesn't mean that it's good for us. You can have perfectly safe food that is devoid of any meaningful nutritional value. Studies have shown that many common illnesses and diseases can be traced back to a lack of nutrition and trace minerals, rather than the presence of toxins (see Chapter Eight). The methods

1   "Farm Operator Household Income Compares Favorably With All U.S. Households, But Varies by Geography and Size of Farm," *Rural Conditions and Trends* 7, no. 1 (1997), http://www.ers.usda.gov/publications/rcat/rcat73/rcat73i.pdf.

of large scale industrial agriculture can deplete the soil of micronutrients by using chemical fertilizers that add nothing to the soil and by
using Roundup which ties up the few nutrients that are in the soil!

Unsustainable Farming Methods

The industrial methods that are used to produce most of our food
are unsustainable. This means that eventually there will come a time
when we can no longer farm as we do today. Greed and a disregard for
God's design in creation have caused the erosion of our soil and the
depletion of its nutrients. We are also very dependent on imported oil
for crop production. We need oil to manufacture the machinery, oil to
run the machinery, oil to fertilize the crops, and oil to harvest them
and transport them. Such a wasteful system could eventually run out of
resources and we would certainly be faced with a food shortage.

Fragile, Centralized Production

Years ago most local regions produced a lot of the food they consumed.
Nowadays in the U.S. hardly any region produces the food they consume. Even if a region primarily produces food, they normally export it
to another region and buy their food from yet another. Iowa is considered the nation's breadbasket and is the nation's leader in production
of major agricultural products such as corn, soybeans, pork, chicken,
etc. However, the state imports eighty percent of the food the people
there eat![2] This dependence on transportation and specialization results in a fragile system of food supply that could easily be interrupted
by the slightest disturbance.

---

2   James Miner, "A Side Order of Sustainability?," The Tomorrow Plan, accessed February 8,
2012, http://www.thetomorrowplan.com/exchange/a-side-order-of-sustainability/

IDOLATROUS AGRICULTURE

As a Christian, I believe that the ultimate root of the problems with American agriculture isn't industrial agriculture. It's not government intervention. It's not imported oil. No, the problem with agriculture today is sin. Specifically, *idolatry*. Man's worship of creation rather than the Creator has resulted in the judgment that is promised.

Modern agriculture is based upon pagan worldviews. If you go to an agricultural college today the methods that are being taught are developed primarily by those who deny God or act as though He doesn't have anything to do with farming. The worship of creation and an evolutionary bias affects the thinking of practically all farming research.

IDOLIZING MAN: THE INDUSTRIAL MODEL

Industrialists worship man and look to godless science (as opposed to God-centered science) to show them how to farm. Industrialism is just today's manifestation of man's ancient idolatry of seeking happiness though materialism, rather than God. So they use technology-based production systems that are designed to efficiently produce cheap "stuff" through centralization, specialization, and standardization. As a result, industrial agriculture views a farm as a factory for the efficient production of large quantities of food through economy of scale and mechanization. This view is backed up and aided by the government who guarantees the success of these methods through subsidies.

The problems of modern agriculture stem from the industrialist's view that the primary goal of agriculture is yield, production, and quantity. "Get the land to produce the greatest amount of food you can in the most efficient manner possible." This results in:

- a scale that makes it hard to be profitable unless you farm *big* time (which typically means loads of debt)

- a farming lifestyle that few people desire

- an emphasis on producing quantity at the expense of quality

- consumption of an unsustainable amount of fuel and soil

- a fragile, centralized network of agricultural production and distribution.

Of course, not everything about industrial agriculture is wrong. It's just that such a narrow objective of high yields has caused some serious side effects. In a word, industrial agriculture tends to be fruitful at the expense of being sustainable.

IDOLIZING NATURE: THE ENVIRONMENTALIST MODEL

The knee jerk reaction then for many of us is to say, "The solution must be sustainable, environmental agriculture!" The term "sustainable" refers to caring for, preserving, and protecting the land's resources. It makes sense that if many of agriculture's problems stem from greedily wasting the land's resources, then the alternative would be to try to care for the land sustainably. And that is true in a sense, but it's an incomplete view that can actually lead us to another extreme that is rooted in idolatry—the extreme of being sustainably unfruitful.

Environmentalists worship creation and look to nature to show them how to farm. Environmentalism is today's manifestation of the idolatry of seeking happiness through the worship of nature and the related concepts of many eastern mystical religions. The underlying goal for agriculture is to be as sustainable as possible, making minimal impact on the land and leaving everything as natural as possible. Environmental farmers rely on the wisdom of nature and the subsidies of the government for their success.

Because environmentalists worship the creation and recognize wisdom in "nature's" design, they tend to have better farming methods than the industrialists. Many of their farms are incredible examples of productive stewardship! However, they attribute the marvel of creation's design to natural processes. As this view becomes more prevalent and applied, I believe we will begin to see a different set of problems arise because man is viewed as part of nature, rather than the steward of it as God intended. The environmentalist's concept of an ideal landscape is one devoid of people. This is reflected in policies like the United Nations' goal of moving everyone into cities and making most everything else "wilderness areas."[3]

CONSEQUENCES

Of the two views, industrialism has been the most destructive because it tends to disregard the wisdom of God's design in creation, and greedily consumes the resources God has given us for the sake of production. Man is viewed as smart enough to manipulate creation unnaturally to his own advantage. As the current leading worldview of agriculture, industrialism is responsible for the majority of the problems we see in agriculture today. Industrial farming is incredibly fruitful, but unsustainable. However, I don't believe that environmentalism offers a complete solution because it promotes a form of sustainability that can result in unfruitfulness. As an example, talk to the farmers in the western states who have livestock being preyed upon by "protected" wolves who were purposely reintroduced to promote "sustainability".

We as Christian farmers tend to take sides with either the industrial or the environmental views. And both have an element of truth to them. Isn't it good to be fruitful? Yes. Isn't it good to be sustainable? Yes. But I believe that for our dirt to be born-again, it must be both sustainable *and* fruitful.

SUSTAINABLY FRUITFUL

When God first gave the assignment of caring for His creation to man and placed him in the garden, the instructions He gave him were to care for and work it (Genesis 2:15). Man's management was to be sustainably fruitful.

Sustainable refers to man's job to protect, maintain, tend, and help supply the needs of the resources he is caring for. He's not supposed to use up or destroy the resources of creation for his own benefit because

---

3 (www.propertyrightsresearch.org/articles2/wildlands_projects_and_un_convention.htm)

he realizes that creation doesn't belong to him. He is responsible for caring for it out of love for God and service to others. Therefore, born-again farmers should seek to maintain and preserve creation for the benefit of future generations.

Fruitful refers to man's job to fully utilize creation for increased productivity. Just as the parable of the talents teaches, man is not simply to *preserve* the "talents" of creation, but is to put them to work to produce fruit.

In agriculture it's easier to be either just "sustainable" or just "fruitful":

- It's easier to be sustainable if we primarily seek to preserve our resources and produce only what it takes to live. However, that is wasting the potential fruitfulness of the land that could be used to serve others.

- Being fruitful is easier if we're only concerned with producing all we can with all the resources we can grab. However, this is robbing future generations of what they need to be fruitful.

As Christian farmers we need to guard against greed. Greed can cause us to pursue riches and farm at the expense of others. And greed can cause us to selfishly produce only what we need while wasting resources that could be used to share with others.

If we want to have born-again dirt then we need to seek to farm in a way that is sustainability fruitful. It's a lot easier to be either sustainable or fruitful. But because it's not about us, we need to purpose to be both sustainable *and* fruitful. Sustainably fruitful is the harder path, but anything less is bad stewardship.

MOVING FORWARD, NOT BACKWARD

When we understand the problems of modern agriculture, we may think, "We just need to get back to the good old days and farm like people used to!" However, we need to recognize that in the past there were good farmers and poor farmers. If we value farming standards of the past merely because they are "old," then we are in danger of forsaking faulty modern standards for faulty old ones.

Someone once said, "Just because something is new, doesn't mean it's better. And just because something is old, doesn't mean it's obsolete." So true. However, the reverse is also true: just because something is old doesn't mean it's better, and just because something is new doesn't mean it's always inferior to the way people used to do it.

In the past, many farming methods tended to stray from Biblical, sustainable fruitfulness. In America, for instance, many of the early Indians were sustainable, but they were not very fruitful. They just existed from one generation to the next, rarely leaving more to the next generation. The European settlers, although Christians, tended to be very fruitful, but not very sustainable. They established a pattern of using up the land and moving west, ruining the inheritance of their descendents.

The solution to the problems with modern agriculture isn't just to return to the way things were done in the past. The solution to the problems of modern agriculture is to establish a Biblical foundation for our agriculture and to seek to apply it in every area of our farming. We need to study and learn from both old and new forms of agriculture through the lens of Scripture. If we seek His truth the Lord can enable us to be more faithful in the area of stewardship than previous generations.

JUDGE NOT—WORK IN PROGRESS!

Please understand that the goal of this chapter was not to discourage anyone who is involved in industrial agri-business. The Lord can use us wherever we are. Whether we are a large scale grain farmer, a small scale organic farmer, or a backyard gardener, the goal is to be ever improving our farms to be more and more God-honoring. Because of sin we will never fully arrive, but we want to be heading in the direction God wants us to go. If large numbers of American farmers made radical, impractical changes overnight, millions of people could starve. The changes that need to be made must be made with care and prayer over a reasonable period of time. Don't let the current place God has you in your journey discourage you from pressing on. Be faithful with the talents the Lord has entrusted to you at this time.

Let's also be careful not to judge others who are in a different stage of the journey. We need to be bold in stating God's principles, but humble and full of grace in considering their application. Let's focus on encouraging one another in the journey and being faithful to press hard after Christ.

4

THE BORN-AGAIN DIRT FARM

What does God want our farms to look like?

ALRIGHT, SO IF GOD PUT US ON THE EARTH TO BE STEWARDS OF IT AND care for and work it, what exactly should the result look like? What should be the characteristics of our farms or gardens? What should be the difference between the wilderness parts of the earth and the parts we tend?

This was probably a question Adam had when God first gave him the job of ruling over the earth.

> God—"Adam, I want you to be fruitful, to multiply and fill the earth, to subdue it, and to rule over all the creatures."
>
> Adam—"Great! But what exactly do you want me to do? I mean, your world is so wonderful, what else am I supposed to do to it?"
>
> God—"Yes, it *is* wonderful, but it's been designed to benefit from your care and management. And don't worry, I will give you an example and you can get some ideas from it. Come, let me show you the garden I just planted."

In my opinion we can't have a better example of what our farms or gardens should look like than the garden God planted Himself. Let's look at the description of the Garden of Eden in Genesis.

> "Now the LORD God had planted a garden in the east, in Eden; and *there he put the man* he had formed. And the LORD God made all kinds of trees grow out of the ground—trees that were *pleasing to the eye* and *good for food*. In the middle of the garden were the tree

33

of life and the tree of the knowledge of good and evil." (Genesis
2:8–9)

So what were the characteristics of the garden God planted? What
were the attributes that man was supposed to imitate in taking dominion of the rest of creation? Here are three major attributes of the
garden of Eden that I believe should define a Christian farm.

1. A Christian's Farm Should Be a Home

The biggest difference between the garden of Eden and the rest of the
"un-gardened" creation was the fact that it had man dwelling in it and
tending it. It wasn't just a beautiful place to grow food, it was a home,
a place to live. A place where man walked with God, worked, and spent
time with his family.

I believe our farms should be homes that are beautiful and fruitful,
not just workplaces where we also live. Many times our farms can take
over our lives because we never leave our work and go home. We tend
to work all the time because we live where we work. However, as good
as work is, our lives are to be primarily relationship-oriented (God and
people), not work-oriented. Therefore, we should view our farms as,
first and foremost, our homes, and not a production factory where we
live.

2. A Christian's Farm Should Be Beautiful

When God planted the garden of Eden, He didn't just go for function.
It says that He planted trees that were pleasing to the eye. This garden
was to reflect the beauty of God Himself, as well as be a pleasant place
for man to live. Our farms should do the same. They should be the
most beautiful farms in the world.

It *is* true that many times on a farm it's "function over form," but
sometimes we can go too far in that direction. We are not just trying
to crank out production with the least amount of effort regardless of
what it looks like (or smells like). We need to care for creation as God
cares for it. And we need to do it with all our heart, displaying our love
for God in the very aesthetics of the land we tend.

3. A Christian's Farm Should Be Fruitful

In addition to being beautiful, we see in the passage above that God planted trees in the garden that were good for food. These were not just ornamental. They grew the food that was needed for man. In this way God displayed His provision and care for Adam and Eve. They, in turn, were able to gain the satisfaction of nurturing the trees and eating the fruit of their efforts.

God has given us an abundance of resources in His creation. Our farms need to reflect that abundance by utilizing those resources. So often our farms waste so many resources and end up being unprofitable. Christian farms, however, should be more productive and fruitful than other farms because they recognize, with thankfulness, the provision of God in creation and waste nothing.

THE PURPOSE OF OUR FARMS

The fact that Eden was a beautiful, fruitful home communicates the purpose of the garden. Our farms should be beautiful, fruitful homes in order that they may accomplish the following:

1. Reflect the Glory of the Creator

Psalms 96 and 148 state that creation declares and reflects God's glory. Well, if the wild parts of creation do that, I believe that a farm tended by a Christian farmer should be a showcase for the attributes of God as displayed in the things He has made (Romans 1:20). This is the reason a farm should be beautiful, fruitful, and habitable. This displays God's splendor, abundance, and love.

A farm is not primarily a showcase of plants and animals, but a showcase of the masterpiece of God's creation, man. God wants us to reflect His image by displaying the same creativity and care in managing His creation that He did in making it. In this way we fulfill the greatest commandment, loving the Lord with all our hearts, worshiping Him by obeying His commands and seeking to be like Him.

2. Provide a Practical Environment for Loving Relationships

The fact that the first farm, or garden, was a place to live, a home, indicates that the purpose of a farm is more than just to grow food. It's to be a place where relationships take place. An agrarian lifestyle provides many opportunities for the cultivation of relationships, both with God and man.

In Genesis, after the account of the fall of man, we are told that God walked in the garden in the cool of the evening. I can imagine that He had previously taken those walks with Adam and Eve, showing them the wisdom of His design in a gecko's feet, or a hummingbird's wing, and sharing about Himself. I believe that God still wants to walk in our gardens and farms with us. There are plenty of opportunities on a farm to pray, sing, and recite, even memorize Scripture while you work! We just need to do a better job of taking advantage of those opportunities.

Adam and Eve also spent time together in the garden, because we are told that when Eve ate the forbidden fruit, "she gave some to her husband also, who was with her." It's sad to see that, instead of using their time together to serve the Lord and love each other, they instead corrupted each other. We are no better. However, we have Christ and He has given us the ability to love each other again. We are told, "By this they will know that you are my disciples, that you love one another" (John 13:34–35). Farming gives us an opportunity to display the gospel by showing love to those around us.

FARM DESIGN

Let's get practical. If God wants our farms to be beautiful, fruitful homes, then how can we design our farms accordingly?

1. Designing for Habitability

How can we design our farms to be homes that are good places to live and work?

There are many ways, but I want to share one that has been helpful to me. It's the principle of designing a *home-centered farm*.

A home-centered farm is set up where the home, or main dwelling, is the center of farm operations. As a result, everything is placed at an appropriate distance from the homes based on the frequency of maintenance and care required. The more often you need to visit something, the closer you put it to the house, and the less frequently you visit it, the further away you place it. In this way you aren't wasting time running all the way across the farm twice a day, 730 times a year to feed chickens.

When you are designing a home-farm you need to consider the fact that farms need to be easily managed. A home-centered farm will have things like intensive gardens, chickens, workshops and barns closest to the house. Beyond that you would have orchards, field crops, and pasture. And outside of that you would have managed semi-wilderness areas. In permaculture this type of planning is referred to as *zone* planning.

The development of a home-centered farm also needs to focus on first getting the area closest to the house under control and then moving outward, being faithful with little before taking on more.

2. Designing for Beauty

There are lots of books that have been written about landscape design and such, but in order to stay simple and try to draw our wisdom from the Lord, the most practical way I know of to design a beautiful farm is *to have diversity of plants and animals.*

When I look at creation, I think it's beautiful. And the most beautiful places to me are the ones with the most abundant diversity of plants and animals. I believe that a flourishing landscape of trees and meadows with birds and beasts best reflects the beauty, creativity, and wisdom of God. A farm with a diversity of plants and animals is more beautiful than a farm that grows just one crop. (It's also more fruitful—but more on that later.)

When we read in Genesis that God planted the trees in the garden of Eden, we see that it says He planted *all kinds of trees*. This wasn't just a pine tree farm (like the many we have near our farm here in Alabama), but this was a farm with a diversity of trees and, I believe, all the plants and wildlife that come with trees, such as vines, shrubs, grasses, birds, squirrels, etc.

Let us consider how we can increase the beauty of our farms by adding more of the beauty of God's creation. I try to plant flowers in my garden, not just for the practical benefit they provide, but also for beauty. It also makes it a more pleasant place to work.

3. Designing for Fruitfulness

The resources God has placed at our disposal in creation are amazing. However, if we fail to recognize and apply some of the basic design principles of creation, we can be very unfruitful. Let's look at some basic design principles and practical applications.

RELATIONAL LOCATION

This principle refers to the idea of locating the different elements of our farms with regard to how they relate to each other. God has designed His creation to function within systems of relationships, where different parts benefit from one another by producing what the other needs, and using what the other produces. If we observe these relationships and seek to implement them in our farm layout, then we will be getting maximum leverage from our resources.

However, for these relationships to work, everything on our farms needs to be placed in the *right* place. We can begin to determine what these places are if we consider both the inputs and outputs of each element and see how they match up with others. Then things that might otherwise be viewed as a liability can become an asset.

Let's look at two elements of my farm, the chickens and the garden, and see how their relationship can increase fruitfulness. Earlier this year I had two problems. First, the pasture that I had planned on keeping my laying chickens in didn't have enough grass. We had cleared the pasture that winter and the grass we had planted hadn't come up very well because of the cold. I knew that the scratching of the chickens would probably kill it. Second, my garden was overgrown with crabgrass, and since it had gone to seed I was overwhelmed with how to get rid of the crabgrass. I also needed to increase the fertility of the garden.

As I was pondering these problems, the Lord finally removed the scales from my eyes and I felt a little silly at the simplicity of the solution. Move the chickens to the garden! We have portable electric fencing that I manage the chickens with and could use it to keep them only in the part of the garden I wanted. I moved them into the weediest part. Since I did, I have found the benefits are amazing. Here are a few of them:

- The chickens turn one of the garden's greatest liabilities, weeds, into one of the garden's greatest assets, fertilizer., The chickens work to clean up weeds and crop residue and turn them into eggs, which we then eat and sell!

- Tillage is minimized to preparing a seed bed and shallow cultivation of weeds. Earthworm population has increased.

- Bug population is kept under control.

- Spoiled produce can be fed to chickens to be converted into eggs and fertilizer.

- No time is required to spread manure

- No time is spent cleaning out coops.

- As the chickens defacate, organic matter can be incorporated into the soil without the danger of losing nitrogen.

- The cost of production of eggs is decreased because the feed bill is less and the fertilizer bill is less.

All these benefits came about because the chickens' outputs (scratching and manure) supplied the garden's inputs. The garden's outputs (greens, bugs, and veggies) supplied the chickens' inputs. None of this would have happened if they hadn't been located based on their relationship.

MULTIFUNCTION EVERYTHING

Another way that we can design our farms for increased fruitfulness is to view everything as having more than one function. God is so abundant and creative that it's hard to find anything in His creation that doesn't produce more than one benefit. We tend to look at only one function that something performs (chickens for eggs, apple tree for fruit, etc.). However, we waste the other functions that those things were created to do. If we want our farms to be fruitful, then we need to seek to identify and utilize as many of the benefits of the different elements of our farm as possible.

For example, let's look at a tree. Normally we plant trees based on one thing we want from them, such as fruit or wood. However, there are many more things that we could be taking advantage of.

- Shade, for livestock or dwellings

- Transpiration, for cooling and humidifying

- Leaves, for mulch and compost

- Habitat, for beneficial birds and animals

- Pruning, for fuel or crafts

- Nitrogen fixing (in select trees)

PERENNIALS FOR FRUITFULNESS
In the garden of Eden we read that God planted perennial trees, not just annual vegetables like most of us plant in our gardens. Utilizing perennials is something we should consider implementing in our designs. Perennials offer many benefits, including multifunction (i.e., produces mulch from leaves and fuel from prunings), less disturbance of the soil, only having to plant them once, and often valuable (and easy to sell) fruits.

The primary reason I planted this year's wheat field is for the wheat. However, it's also serving as ground cover to prevent erosion, a green plot for deer hunting, and winter grazing for our animals. After we harvest and thresh the wheat, the straw can also be used for mulch or bedding.

For maximum fruitfulness our farms need to be designed with as much multifunction productivity as possible.

MULTIPLE SUPPORTING SYSTEMS *(don't put all your eggs in one basket)*

If we want our farms to be fruitful, then we need to make sure that the needs of each element are supported by more than one source. As

Christian farmers we don't farm in pre-fall Eden. We farm in a world full of sin that is groaning under the effects of the curse. Therefore, it's unwise (actually, foolish) to plan on everything always going perfectly. Something, at some point, is going to mess up and fail. Plants and animals get sick and die, extremes of weather cause droughts, floods, and tornadoes, and machinery will break down.

With that in mind, it's wise when trying to meet the needs of the flora and fauna (plants and animals) of our farm to try to have more than one source of something—so that when one source fails (and it *will* fail at some point) we can still meet needs. One backup is better than none, but three is even *better*. Ecclesiastes 4:12 says, "A cord of *three* strands is not easily broken."

Water is a good example. Life on a farm is pretty dependent on water, so have as many sources as you can. On our farm we are extremely blessed to have five different sources: rain water, pond water, creek and spring water, well water, and city water. With all of these it's *very* unlikely that we will run out of water. For instance, in Alabama our plumbing and water spigots aren't very freeze-proof because it doesn't get cold very often. When it does freeze, it normally gets warm enough during the day to thaw the lines. However, a few times a winter it will stay cold enough during the day that the chickens run out of water. So, during those times we haul water from the pond in buckets.

Other examples of needs that should have multiple sources might be animal feed (such as buying it, growing it, and letting animals forage), soil fertility (green manure crops, animal manures, mulches), and tools (hand tool alternatives to power tools).

NO WASTED RESOURCES

In order to be fruitful, our farms need to be designed to take advantage of and utilize every resource so there is no waste. If we are wasteful we aren't going to be as profitable and fruitful as we could be otherwise. If our farms are wasteful, then they won't be properly displaying God's abundance.

If we want to have farms that are fruitful, then we need to eliminate the word *waste* from our vocabulary. We aren't perfect, so we won't be able to fully utilize everything on our farms but we should give thanks and appreciate things as much as possible. We can easily become so shortsighted and get so focused on what we want to get out of our farm that we don't value many of the other things our farms produce. Instead, they are labeled "waste" and thrown away.

Waste is misplaced resources. In order to design fruitful farms we need to look at all the potential waste products, and find a way to use them. Weeds and spoiled vegetables can be used to feed chickens. Whey from cheese making can be used to feed pigs. Manure from livestock can be used to feed the garden.

God is not a God of waste. He is a God of abundance. Although sin has corrupted creation, it's hard to find anything that is completely useless. As stewards we need to try and take everything produced by our farm and use it to produce something beautiful, or useful.

WHAT IS A FARM?

Some of you are probably reading this and thinking, "But I don't have a farm, I just have a yard and a few raised beds!" Well, here's my definition of a farm: *A farm is a piece of land—regardless of size—that an individual is responsible for.*

According to this definition, if you own or rent or are otherwise responsible for a piece of land, however large or small, you have a farm. You are therefore responsible to make that land a beautiful and fruitful home. In my opinion, this means that if you have an ornamental lawn, you should at least plant something that will grow some food and put some pathways through it so that it's inviting to people.

Even if you live in an apartment, I would encourage you to get a few potted plants, or a window box planter. This gives you the opportunity to steward some dirt, even if you don't own "land." See if you can make your portable farm beautiful and fruitful.

CONCLUSION

If we want our farms to be born-again, a good place to start would be to copy the characteristics of the garden of Eden. We should seek to have farms that are beautiful, fruitful homes.

The main difference between wilderness and a garden is the presence of man. It's a place where man dwells and walks with God. Man was created to work the ground, and the ground was designed to be worked by man. Genesis 2:4–5 says, "When the LORD God made the earth and the heavens and no shrub of the field had yet appeared on the earth and no plant of the field had yet sprung up, for the LORD God had not sent rain on the earth and *there was no man to work the ground....*"

Many people would have us believe that nature is in its perfect and best state as wilderness, and any intrusion by man is a blight on the landscape. However, although the "unsubdued" parts of nature were declared "good" by God at the end of the creation week, man and his role to work and care for the earth was also declared good. Wilderness is good, but its design and intent was that it should be improved by man's proper management. Isaiah 45:18 declares, "For this is what the Lord says—he who created the heavens, he is God; he who fashioned and made the earth, he founded it; *he did not create it to be empty, but formed it to be inhabited*" (emphasis mine).

Although I am still working on applying all the principles shared in this chapter on my own farm, I can testify that a born-again farm is a great place to live. Because it's designed to be a beautiful, fruitful home, it's a joy to go out and work every day. There are still days, as I progress in the journey, that I have to purpose to be thankful, but I wouldn't trade my "office" or "co-workers" with any others in the world. I pray that as our farms become more beautiful, fruitful, and habitable, the world will begin looking to us to tell them the secrets of our farms. Then we can point them to Christ.

5

THE ROLE OF A CHRISTIAN FARMER

Being good and faithful stewards of the land.

IF WE WANT TO HAVE BORN-AGAIN DIRT, THEN WE MUST BEGIN TO TAKE seriously our job as stewards. It's not enough to just acknowledge God's ownership of our farms. We must also accept our responsibility to manage them in the way He wants.

This chapter is a particularly convicting one for me to write, because I am the farm manager of our family's farm. Even as I did the chores this morning, I saw so many areas of neglect and poor management on our farm. I have so far to go to be a good steward and I need the strength of Christ to enable me. I need to surrender my time to Him, acknowledging that it, and my farm, belong to Him.

This chapter is *partly* about what we as farmers should do, but it's *mostly* about what we are supposed to *be*. God doesn't just care about what we do and how we do it, He cares about our hearts.

> *It's not enough to just acknowledge God's ownership of our farms; we must also accept our responsibility to manage them in the way He wants.*

In the last chapter I stated that if you have dirt, you have a farm and are a farmer. The potential for bringing glory to God though biblical land management is immense, and every Christian with dirt needs to seek to be a good steward.

OUR JOB AS CHRISTIAN FARMERS

God created the world and everything in it. He is the owner of everything and has entrusted, not given, His creation to the care of man. As farmers we are merely stewards of the land, those who have been entrusted with the property of another.

Our job as stewards is to manage the land in a way that is sustainably fruitful. Caring for and working it was Adam's job in the garden of Eden.

So if our job as stewards is to care for and work the land, what does that look like? How can we apply that on our farms? Let's look at a few examples.

CARING FOR THE LAND

In order to properly care for our farms as Christian farmers we must be:

Faithful in the Maintenance of Our Farms

In Scripture we see many passages that warn against failing to maintain and care for what you have. One of my favorites is the one about the sluggard's vineyard.

> I went past the field of the sluggard, past the vineyard of the man who lacks judgment; thorns had come up everywhere, the ground was covered with weeds, and the stone wall was in ruins. I applied my heart to what I observed and learned a lesson from what I saw: A little sleep, a little slumber, a little folding of the hands to rest— and poverty will come on you like a bandit and scarcity like an armed man. (Proverbs 24:30–34)

It's interesting to note that the fruit of being a sluggard isn't that he didn't have resources, (a vineyard with a wall around it) but that he didn't maintain what he had. This is so often the case with me. I am very good at accumulating resources, but not very good at taking care of the ones I have. In this age of disposable everything, maintenance isn't always as highly valued as it once was. Manufacturers and marketers want us to buy things, use them up, throw them away and buy new ones. They don't want us to take care of what we have.

We need to value the things the Lord has given us because they belong to him, and are a gift from Him. "The lazy man does not roast his game, but the diligent man prizes his possessions" (Proverbs 12:27).

ATTENTIVE TO THE NEEDS OF OUR FARM

If we are going to care for our farms, then we need to be observant and aware of what needs they have. We need to look at all the different elements of our farms as we manage them, searching for and identifying the needs we must try and meet. I know I can easily go about my work, not really paying attention to what things might need my attention and care.

> Be sure you know the condition of your flocks, give careful attention to your herds; for riches do not endure forever, and a crown is not secure for all generations. (Proverbs 27:23–24)

As we see in the verse above, we need to keep tabs on the condition of the different parts of our farm. We shouldn't assume that everything is just going fine and shouldn't assume that it will keep going fine. For instance, I need to do a better job with my the bees. They are in a field that I am not using at this moment for pasture and I have to go and see them to check on their flight activity. Lately, I haven't been up there to check on them like I should to see what they need.

CONSIDERATE AND KIND IN THE CARE OF OUR ANIMALS

> A righteous man cares for the needs of his animal, but the kindest acts of the wicked are cruel. (Proverbs 12:10)

As stewards we have been given dominion over our animals and we must respect the life God has given them. In order to bring glory to God, I believe we should seek to reflect the same care and provision to them that God shows to those under His care. This doesn't mean that we worship them or raise them up to the status of man, but we desire to show the same kindness in our rule of the animals as God does for us. Keeping them supplied with water, providing quality feed, grass or hay, avoiding unnecessary disturbances, and protecting them from the weather and predators are all ways we can show care and respect for the life of our animals. When we do daily chores for our chickens we sometimes call it "going to make the chickens happy". Even when it comes time to 'harvest' our animals for their meat, we attempt to do it in a way that shows respect and gratitude for the life God gave them.

WORKING THE LAND

In order to put our farms to work, as Christian farmers we must be:

DILIGENT AND HARD WORKING

One of the primary ways that our land is worked is through *our* work. If we aren't diligent, if we don't get out there and utilize the resources at hand, then we won't be producing fruit. Work is a good thing, and we aren't going to get anything done if we laze around the farm. The book of Proverbs has a lot to say about work and diligence:

> He who works his land will have abundant food, but he who chases fantasies lacks judgment. (Proverbs 12:11)

> All hard work brings a profit, but mere talk leads only to poverty. (Proverbs 14:23)

It's easy for me to waste a lot of time talking about what I am going to do or planning what I am going to do and never really get anything done. If we want to make a profit, we need to get out and get our hands dirty and sweat some.

If we aren't diligent, if we don't get out there and utilize the resources at hand, then we won't be producing any fruit.

> One who is slack in his work is brother to one who destroys. (Proverbs 18:9)

If we waste time because of lack of diligence and because of laziness, then the resulting slack in our work is just the same as if we had first built something, then destroyed what we had built. If we are going to do something, we need to do it well and not half-done. (Man, am I preaching to myself!)

> Do you see a man skilled in his work? He will serve before kings; he will not serve before obscure men. (Proverbs 22:29)

PROMPT AND TIMELY IN THE TASKS WE PERFORM

If we are going to do a good job of working our land, it's important that we do things in a timely manner. Much labor can be saved and production increased by doing things at the right time. I have found this to be true in many areas. For instance, spinach in our fall garden that was planted on time produced well. A planting done two weeks late produced almost nothing. If I delay pruning tomato plants, then it takes much longer than if I had done it when the plants were younger. Proverbs has many convicting verses about the importance of doing things on time.

> He who gathers crops in summer is a wise son, but he who sleeps during harvest is a disgraceful son. (Proverbs 10:5)

> A sluggard does not plow in season, so at harvest time he looks but finds nothing. (Proverbs 20:4)

Timeliness is an important quality of God's character, and is reflected in His creation. God never does anything too soon, or too late. Everything He does is right on time. We see much evidence of the importance of timeliness in creation. The sun always rises and sets on time. Seeds must germinate at the right time of year to thrive. Animals must mate at particular times to produce offspring. If timeliness was abandoned in creation tomorrow, everything would fall apart.

As stewards, we must reflect and honor the timeliness of God and His creation in the way we manage it. It matters when you do something.

Ecclesiastes 8:6 tells us that there is a proper time and procedure for every matter. We need to ask God to help us determine the proper time for doing things and then be punctual. Plant those seeds when you are supposed to. Change the oil in the tractor when you are supposed to. Put bedding in the nesting boxes before they get too dirty. It's not easy. These are all things I struggle with doing on time. With Christ working though us, we can do all He calls us to.

Thoughtful and Wise to Plan Ahead

Today the world tells us to follow our hearts. In movies and other media people who make decisions based on what they "feel" are held up as much more enlightened then the fuddy-duddies who carefully plan and make wise decisions. Proverbs 28:26 says, "He who trusts in himself is a fool, but he who walks in wisdom is kept safe."

If we start trusting in our plans rather than in God to make us succeed, then we are idolaters.

As Christian farmers we need to be good stewards of the land through being purposeful to plan and apply what God has told us to do. Otherwise we might be spending our energies doing something counterproductive that would have been obvious if we had planned. "The wisdom of the prudent is to give thought to their ways" (Proverbs 14:8).

Planning allows us to make the best use of the resources of our farms. It allows us to evaluate our farms and consider how we can do a better job of glorifying God in every area. A Christian farmer's responsibility is not to just "hope" his dirt can be born-again, but to "consider his ways" and come up with a practical plan for applying God's principles.

Planning is important for profit. "The plans of the diligent lead to profit, as surely as haste leads to poverty" (Proverbs 21:5). When we started our farm my father had me write a business plan for the farm which, in essence, was a master plan for the farm. Of course, our farm didn't follow that plan exactly, but just going through the process and evaluating production, marketing, income and expense helped me to do a better job of being faithful to put the resources of our farm to work. And it helped me to see ahead of time if something I planned to do had the possibility of being profitable.

Planning is also to be surrendered to the Lord. We can make all the plans we want, and we should plan, but if we start trusting in our plans rather than in God to make us succeed, then we are idolaters. God is sovereign, and no plan can succeed against him. "There is no wisdom, no insight, no plan that can succeed against the LORD" (Proverbs 21:30). Thankfully, we are told that although God wants us to plan as good stewards, He is the one who ultimately guides our steps. "In his heart a man plans his course, but the Lord determines his steps" (Proverbs 16:9).

I am thankful that God doesn't leave the success of my farm up to my own ability to plan. I would be sure to fail if that was the case!

CULTIVATING A PROPER HEART

In order to be a faithful steward, a Christian farmer needs to have the right heart. "The good man brings good things out of the good stored up in his heart, and the evil man brings evil things out of the evil stored up in his heart" (Luke 6:45).

Lets look at a few heart qualities that are important for a Christian farmer to have.

THANKFULNESS

One of the notable characteristics of most farmers is the tendency to gripe and complain about their farm: the wet weather that kept them from planting, the dry weather that dried up their crops, the tractor that broke down, the cow that got sick, the poor prices. For a Christian farmer, complaining is wrong. It's a sin to complain (Philippians 2:14).

Christian farmers must cultivate a heart of thankfulness. There is never a time when a farmer doesn't have something to be thankful for. In fact, there is nothing that a farmer has to be ungrateful for! 1 Thessalonians 5:18 says, "Give thanks in all circumstances, for this is God's will for you in Christ Jesus." I want to be known as the grateful farmer, the farmer who doesn't complain.

Many times we farmers don't realize the full potential of our farms because we waste so much time being ungrateful that we miss all the abundance of blessing that God bestows on us.

JOY

The result of thankfulness should be joy. Whenever I am working and feel myself getting depressed because things aren't going right, I try to begin to give thanks to the Lord. When I do, it often brings me a joy that is unexplainable according to my circumstances.

As Christians our joy is found in the Lord Jesus Christ. We can be joyful even if our farms go kaput tomorrow. We have a very clear example of this in Scripture.

> Though the fig tree does not bud and there are no grapes on the vines, though the olive crop fails and the fields produce no food, though there are no sheep in the pen and no cattle in the stalls, yet I will rejoice in the Lord, I will be joyful in God my Savior. (Habakkuk 3:17–18)

I recently memorized this passage and would highly recommend all Christian farmers to do so. It's a very helpful reminder to recite it when things aren't going as you want.

Another passage I would recommend that you memorize is 1 Thessalonians 5:16–18.

> Be joyful always, pray continually, give thanks in all circumstances, for this is God's will for you in Christ Jesus.

This passage can help keep you in a grateful, joyful attitude while you work.

HUMILITY

If we are going to be good stewards of the land God has given us, then we need to be humble. To be successful farmers we need wisdom, and wisdom comes from humility (Proverbs 11:2). The times that I have failed the most are when I was being prideful and sought neither the Lord's wisdom, nor the counsel of the wise.

We also need to be humble in looking at the way we farm and being willing to change. This is one of the hardest challenges—to acknowledge that the way I have been doing something might not be the best way and to work to change it.

It's also easy for me to be prideful because I am trying to farm differently than most people. I might begin to think that I know more than others do. However, I am practically in farming kindergarten compared to most farmers and need to swallow my pride and realize that God can share wisdom through them, even if I wouldn't adopt their practices.

WHOLEHEARTEDNESS

As farmers who work for the Lord, we need to do everything wholeheartedly. We are commanded to love God with our whole heart, and farming is an expression of love and obedience to God. This isn't something we do for ourselves in which we can be careless if we want to. This is our act of worship to the Lord!

> Whatever you do, work at it with all your heart, as working for the Lord, not for men. (Colossians 3:23)

Wholeheartedness flows from a heart that passionately loves the Lord and wants to serve and bring glory to him. When we care for our farms, we shouldn't hold anything back. We should go all out farming for God—not in the sense that we are workaholics or to abuse our bodies. We should have a zeal that drives us to go above and beyond the call of duty. Often I find myself going about my work, doing only what has to be done. Jesus illustrates in the following passage that we are unworthy as servants and stewards if we halfheartedly go about our duty.

> So you also, when you have done everything you were told to do, should say, 'We are unworthy servants; we have only done our duty.' (Luke 17:10)

———

The preceding heart qualities certainly don't cover every aspect of the heart that we as Christian farmers need to have, but they provide a starting place and hopefully will help us begin to see the other areas of our hearts that impact our farming. We need to remember that only Christ can change our hearts. We need to go to the Lord in prayer and ask Him to give us the hearts He wants us to have.

TRUSTING IN GOD THROUGH FAITHFUL (NOT FRANTIC) WORK

As I try to be a good steward, I struggle to determine how much work I should get done each day. My tendency is to look at all that I want to get done, write up an optimistic "to do" list for the day, and then run around frantically trying to get it all done. At the end of the day I'm usually disappointed because I didn't do it all. I don't think this is what God desires for His farmers.

One of the biblical foundations for born-again dirt that we looked at earlier is the fact that God is the one Who makes things grow. In other words, only He can produce the fruit. This means that we aren't to go out and try to produce fruit in our own strength. Instead, we need to focus on being faithful with the time, skill, and resources God has given us and leave the results of our faithfulness up to Him.

God gives us enough time during the day to get done all that He wants us to do, but not necessarily all that we want to do.

My disappointment when I don't get "everything" done that I want to get done is primarily due to my unrealistic expectations. I am try-ing to do more than God has given me time, talent, and resources to do. Because God always provides us a way to do what He commands, I know that there is enough time in the day to get done what He wants me to do. If I don't have enough time, then I am obviously trying to do more than God expects for me that day. I need to evaluate what I have on my list and pray that God would help me to know what things are important to Him.

> Unless the LORD builds the house, its builders labor in vain. Un-less the LORD watches over the city, the watchmen stand guard in vain. In vain you rise early and stay up late, toiling for food to eat—for he grants sleep to those he loves. (Psalm 128:1–2)

Frantic work indicates that I am being greedy and striving to achieve things in my own strength or that I'm just being lazy because I want to get done quickly and move on to other things instead of enjoying the work the Lord has given me. If I am trusting in the Lord to bless the work of my hands, then my work won't be a *frantic* working.

> Do not love sleep or you will grow poor; stay awake and you will have food to spare. (Proverbs 20:13)

If we aren't getting enough sleep, it is an indication that we are trying to do too much. There is a time for sleep and a time to be awake and work.

Instead of frantic work, I think that Christian farmers should manage their farms through faithful work. I have found this to be much more peaceful and less stressful. What I mean by faithful work is that instead of going out with a list of what I want to get done and making the main objective to accomplish as much work as possible, I try to prayerfully put together my list for the day and faithfully complete each chore to the best of my ability. This needs to be done with a sensitivity to the Holy Spirit for other opportunities that arise. At the end of the day, if I know that I was faithful to be diligent, working wholeheartedly at caring for and working my land, then I can be content because I accomplished what God wanted me to. Of course, there are times to press hard and work 'round the clock, but I don't believe it should be the norm. First Thessalonians 4:11–12 talks about leading a quiet life, which would indicate peaceful and contented work, rather than stressful, frustrating work.

As stewards let us guard against greed and striving to succeed in our own strength by frantic working. Instead, let us rest in the provision of God and wholeheartedly pursue faithfulness in caring for and working our land during the hours of the day He gives us.

PRACTICAL IDEAS FOR STEWARDSHIP

WALK YOUR FARM WITH *THE* OWNER

One thing that could help promote a better sense of stewardship in our hearts is taking a walk around the farm. The goal of the walk is not to dwell on the work you need to do on the farm, but rather to walk the farm with its Owner. Apparently God walked with Adam, the first steward, in the garden of Eden. I think the Lord would enjoy walking with us around the farms He has given us.

On your walk with the Lord go alone if possible. Pray out loud or whisper if that would be more comfortable. Just talk with the Lord and give Him a tour of the farm. Thank Him for all that He has given you. Show Him the garden, the chickens, the pasture, the greenhouse, the cows—whatever you have, and give Him an account of how you have been caring for and working them. Acknowledge that they all belong to Him and ask Him to show you how you can better manage them. When you come across the chickens that are walking around in mud because you have been putting off moving them (because you have been trying to work on writing a book) then repent and ask Him to help you do a better job. Tell Him about the problem you have with disease on your tomato plants, or erosion in your newly planted pasture and ask Him to show you a solution. At times just be silent and observe. Look at His design in creation. Pay attention to the needs that you may have previously overlooked. Take notice of any opportunities that He may reveal to you, like the acorns in the woods that could be fed to the pigs. At the end of the walk give thanks to God for granting you this land and dedicate it to His glory.

Keep a Husbandry Journal

In addition to taking farm walks with the Lord, it's helpful to keep a journal of things He shows you so that they won't be forgotten. You can use it to write down verses you read that pertain to agriculture, ways that you have sought to apply the gospel to your farm, and the ways the Lord has blessed your faithfulness. You could write down prayer requests for your farm (e.g., protect the chickens from predators, help the meat chickens to grow big enough to make a profit, provide a market for the broccoli, etc.) In a sense the journal could be a record of the "sanctification" of your farm. It's also very helpful to keep good farm records as references for faithful planning.

Pray Over Your Crops

One thing that can help guard against farming in our own strength is praying over our crops. In chapter two I told the story of Mr. Hay, who would sit on a log at the edge of his garden after planting and pray that the Lord would bless his work. I have tried to do this myself when

I plant anything, or when I am raising an animal. After putting in a new planting of beans or tomatoes or whatever, I pray that the Lord would bless *His* crop, and make it grow lots of food to feed my family and many others. I also acknowledge that it belongs to Him and if He wants to flatten it with a hailstorm, then He has the right to do that.

When I acknowledge that I am totally dependent on the Lord to succeed and ask for His blessing, then, when He gives it, He gets more glory than if I had just hoped that the work I did would produce fruit. When it does give fruit and you are out there picking beans in the heat of the summer, give thanks for the beans and don't complain! (Try to get out there next time before it gets too hot!)

CONCLUSION

Being a Christian farmer has many benefits. For one thing, there is peace and security for the farmer that he could never find in any crop insurance or government farm bill. When you acknowledge that God is in control, then there is no need to worry. Also, when you work for the Lord there is an accountability and motive for doing your best that couldn't be provided by the strictest inspection program.

Our role as farmers who are born-again, or redeemed by the blood of Christ, is an important one, but it's not an easy one. To embrace the role of a Christian farmer goes against our sinful, selfish nature. If we want to see agriculture renewed, if we want to see a healing of the land that has been torn by the effects of sin, if we want to see an abundance of fruitfulness that can't be matched by other farmers, then we need to surrender to Christ and let Him create new hearts in the farmers of the Church. May God raise up a generation of born-again farmers.

6

PRINCIPLES OF GOD'S DESIGN

What principles should direct our farming methods?

NOW WE ARE FINALLY GETTING TO THE ACTUAL "FARMING" PART OF the book. How do we answer questions like: "When should I plant my tomato plant?", or "What type of chicken coop should I build?" These are the nitty-gritty, everyday questions that we as farmers (or gardeners) are faced with. How should our worldview, the fact that we are born-again, impact how we actually produce food? I'm sorry if it disappoints you, but I don't have all the answers. However, I know the One who *does*.

LEARNING TO FARM FROM THE EXPERT

There are many agricultural experts out there who will be glad to teach you all about farming (often for a handsome fee). But we have to admit that they can't really be experts in agriculture in the sense that they have figured it all out. Material science, physics, and calculus are all pretty complicated, but compared to agriculture they are like preschool.

Some people may say, "But wait a minute, I thought farming was for dummies who couldn't do physics and calculus!" I would argue that agriculture is much more difficult to truly master because it deals with biology, with living organisms.

I admit, working with metal is interesting. I used to have a black-smithing business. Working with wood is great, too. I have also done carpentry. Compare a hunk of metal or a piece of wood, whose properties are generally understandable, to any living organism, even a "simple" cell, and the difference in complexity is incredible. As a farmer, how do we even begin to understand everything that goes into making a plant grow? How can a sheep take grass and turn it into energy, meat, wool, and lambs with the only byproduct of the process being great manure for the grass?

We cannot begin to understand the living creatures and systems in creation well enough to be able to manipulate them as industrial agriculture does today. To treat a chicken like a hunk of metal or wood in a factory denies the value of life that God has given that creature. Metal and wood are dead materials that have simple properties and and can be used as building blocks to make tools and structure that are useful to man. A chicken is a totally different story. It's a living creature that has *already* been designed to perform a specific function within a specific environment. The chicken's Designer was better than any human engineer. God Himself, the source of all wisdom, designed chickens. He knows everything there is to know about everything, past present and future. How much do any of us know compared to that? Basically nothing!

> *I believe that as Christian farmers we should look not primarily to the* WORLD'S *farming experts, but to* THE *farming Expert.*

Therefore, I believe that as Christian farmers we should look not primarily to the *world's* farming experts, but to *the* farming Expert. God can teach us through the experiences and observations of men, but it makes much more sense to base our farming knowledge on wisdom that comes from the One who knows everything about farming, rather than those who know almost nothing.

Many of the farming experts today deny the existence of *the* Expert, and their materialistic, naturalistic presupposition affects their interpretation of what they see in creation. To them, a hunk of metal and a chicken are ultimately both just blobs of molecules, so why not just plug a chicken into an industrial production model? If the chicken came about because of a bunch of random accidents, then it makes sense that by applying our logic and observation we ought to be able to come up with a better way to produce chickens.

If we want to learn from *the* Expert, what do we do? In order to develop God-glorifying production methods for farming *we need to honor the principles we see in the design of creation.* Our production is going to be most successful when we manage creation in a way consistent with its design.

As Christian farmers, we believe that God created everything and that we know practically nothing compared to him. We also believe that He revealed himself to us through the Bible and creation. God created everything good and, although corrupted by sin, His creation displays His wisdom and character (Romans 1:20). Therefore, if we want to have production models that glorify God, then these models need to honor the principles in creation that reflect His wisdom and character. If our methods ignore or violate His ways, then we are denying and dishonoring the very nature of God.

Principles that we observe in creation have to be viewed in light of Scripture. The Bible is the lens that allows us to see the world around us clearly. If something we see in creation is in conflict with the Word of God, then we are not seeing it rightly. Our limited observation doesn't trump the plain, written Word of God.

In this chapter, we are going to look at a few basic principles founded in both Scripture and creation that relate to agricultural production. These principles are:

- Healthy soil results in healthy plants.

- The changing seasons affect plants and animals.

- God created plants and animals to function in certain ways, filling certain roles on the farm.

- God commands us to take time for rest.

This isn't an exhaustive list but it will help us to think about what type of farming methods might be the most God-honoring. We will examine some possible ways these principles can be applied on our farms. In the next chapter we'll look at some patterns that we can apply in plant and animal production.

PRINCIPLE #1: SOIL-BASED

Plant production, upon which animal production is dependent, is founded upon healthy soil.

One of the most foundational elements in the production of living organisms on our farms is soil. Dirt. It really is true that healthy, viable farms start with born-again dirt. Healthy plants, healthy animals, and healthy people all depend upon healthy soil.

SOIL IN SCRIPTURE

I believe we see the principle of the foundation of soil for life many places in Scripture (including the fact that man was formed from soil). Here is a familiar passage:

> "Listen! A farmer went out to sow his seed. As he was scattering the seed, some fell along the path, and the birds came and ate it up. Some fell on rocky places, where it did not have much *soil*. It sprang up quickly, because the *soil* was shallow. But when the sun came up, the plants were scorched, and they withered because they had no root. Other seed fell among thorns, which grew up and choked the plants, so that they did not bear grain. Still other seed fell on good *soil*. It came up, grew and produced a crop, multiplying thirty, sixty, or even a hundred times. (Mark 4:3–8)

What was the difference between the plants that died or produced nothing and the plants that yielded a crop?
IT WAS THE SOIL.

In this parable Jesus is illustrating the receptivity of the gospel in different hearts. Throughout Scripture we see that the heart is what brings forth the good or bad fruit in a person's life. Since Jesus used soil as a representative of the human heart, it should be true that healthy or sickly plants are the result of the soil they grow in. What was the difference between the plants that died or produced nothing and the plants that yielded a crop? *It was the soil.*

Soil in Creation

In creation it's obvious that healthy soil is the basis of healthy plants and animals. Just go out on your farm or in your backyard and look at the difference in the soil where the plants are thriving and the soil where there are few or no plants. In most normal situations the soil where the healthy plants are growing will appear much superior, even if you aren't a dirt expert. The consistency, color, and depth will be richer and there will be a host of small creatures living in it. If you have ever tried to grow a garden, then you know first hand that if you improve the soil of an area, then it will grow much better weeds than the surrounding soil!

Characteristics of Healthy Soil

What does healthy soil look like?

NOT COMPACTED

In the parable of the sower we saw that the compacted soil of the path was not suitable for growing. We also see in creation that plants grow better in soil that is loose, rather than hard. This allows space for water and air in the soil that is necessary for drainage, roots, and soil life. Therefore, good soil should be loose, not compacted.

DEEP

We also see in the parable of the sower that the shallow soil wasn't good because it didn't allow the plants' roots to go deep and they died from lack of water. Deep soil allows the roots of plants to reach down deep and access water in the soil below the drier surface. Deep soil also allows for more water to be stored in the soil rather than running off. Therefore, good soil should be deep.

WEED-FREE

The third place the seed in the parable was sown was among thorns. These weeds competed for water and nutrients and "choked" the plants. Many times weeds don't kill the plants we are growing, but their competition causes them to be unfruitful. Therefore, good soil should be relatively weed-free.

LIVING

Contrary to what most of us would think, good soil isn't just a sterile growing medium that is dark in color. No, if you go look at the rich soil in the woods you will see that it's crawling with life. These microorganisms break down raw materials in the soil and make them available to the plants. Without the life of the soil, plants will not be as healthy as they might be because they can't access very many nutrients. In Scripture we see that life is good, and death is bad, so I believe "good" soil would indicate soil with life in it. Therefore, good soil should be living.

DEVELOPING SOIL-BASED METHODS

What are some ways that our methods could reflect the importance of soil to farming production? Here are a few suggestions.

FOCUS ON BUILDING HEALTHY SOIL

If healthy soil is the way to get healthy plants and animals, then one of the main focuses of our farms should be building healthy soil! Today there are two main approaches to improving the plant producing qualities of your soil.

- FEED THE PLANT: This approach seeks to increase the yield of land by adding soluble chemical fertilizers to the soil that have nutrients that can be directly accessed by the plants.

- FEED THE SOIL: This approach seeks to increase the yield of land by adding soil amendments that feed the soil, so the soil can feed the plant.

The first approach of feeding the plants is what is most commonly promoted in today's agriculture. However, because this isn't consistent with God's design of healthy soil being the foundation of healthy plants, it presents some difficulties. First, soluble chemical fertilizers don't build soil. They tend to be like a drug. The more you use them, the more you *must* use just to get the same effect, and the more difficult it is to stop using them because it takes time for the soil health to build back up. Second, chemical fertilizers can't be produced on the farm and must be bought and imported, which raises the cost of production.

The approach of feeding the soil so it can feed the plants is a much better way to increase the yield of your land. I believe it's more consistent with God's design. It has many benefits. The longer you feed your soil, the less you have to do so. As the health of the soil is increased, it takes less to maintain it. Also, many of the amendments it takes to build healthy soil are available as by-products of other parts of the farm.

Here are a few tips for building healthy soil:

- Use mulches of organic material such as leaves, wood chips, hay, straw, etc.

- Grow leguminous plants and trees that will harbor nitrogen-fixing bacteria in their roots while they grow mulch material.

- Keep the ground covered as much as possible

- Apply manures to the soil (or better yet, let the animals do it)

RECOGNIZE POOR SOIL AS THE CAUSE OF MOST PLANT DISEASES AND PESTS

If healthy soil is the foundation of healthy plants, then we need to view unhealthy plants as the result of unhealthy soil. The most common approach to dealing with disease and pests today is to treat them as the problem. However, if soil is the basis of health, then we should view them as the symptom of the problem, not the source.

For example, if aphids are attacking a plant, many times it's because the plant is stressed and weak. We can try to find a way to discourage and get rid of the aphids, but they aren't the problem. The unhealthy plant is the problem. The way we fix that is by fixing the soil. The aphids are just doing their job. God designed His creation to weed out things that are unhealthy and sick, so if our plants are that way, then we shouldn't be surprised when plant assassins (diseases and pests) show up and start recycling our plants as food.

MANAGE ANIMALS FOR SOIL ENRICHMENT

If we want to have healthy soil, then we need to manage our farm to facilitate building soil. One way we can do this is in the proper management of animals. Plants and animals have been designed to benefit one another. Animals eat parts of plants and, in return, give the plants the nutrients they need to grow by defecating on the soil.

A simple example of this would be having cows eat grass out in the pasture or incorporating chickens in the garden. Both plants and animals are required on your farm, which is ideal in my opinion and more consistent with God's design. Most farms today are so specialized that you typically see all the animals in one area and far away in another area you have all the plants. The manure that could be going towards producing better soil is instead a bothersome by-product. I believe that we can have healthier soil and healthier farms if we use animals in conjunction with plant production.

What About Hydroponics?

Today an increasing number of farmers are beginning to grow plants using hydroponics. Plants are grown in nutrient rich water instead of soil. Does this violate the principle of having soil-based production? I would tend to disagree with anyone who says that growing plants hydroponically is superior to growing them in soil, but I think it's a perfectly legitimate and very creative way to grow things. It's especially useful in situations that allow you to use waste from fish production or grow plants where you normally wouldn't be able to. But the ease of such automated systems does not carry with it the same "forgiveness" in production that soil-based agriculture does.

PRINCIPLE #2: SEASONAL

Another major principle that should impact our production is the fact that cycles and processes of life are designed to function within a system of seasons. Plant and animal production is best when done according to the appropriate seasons. Seasons regulate when plants grow, when flowers bloom, when animals mate, when seeds sprout, etc. In managing the production of living creatures, we should take into account the importance of doing things according to seasons.

SEASONS IN SCRIPTURE

The Bible talks a lot about seasons. Let's draw a few observations from various verses:

GOD CREATED SEASONS

> And God said, "Let there be lights in the expanse of the sky to separate the day from the night, and let them serve as signs to mark *seasons* and days and years. (Genesis 1:14)

From the beginning of creation we see that there were seasons that ordered nature. These reflect the order and faithfulness of God. After the flood, God promised that as long as the earth endured there would be seasons. (Genesis 8:22)

THERE IS A SEASON FOR EVERYTHING

> There is a time for everything, and a *season* for every activity under heaven. (Ecclesiastes 3:1)

> For there is a *proper time* and procedure for every matter. (Ecclesiastes 8:6a)

Seasons help regulate our activities. Apparently, there are times better suited to doing certain things than other times.

IT'S IMPORTANT TO DO THINGS IN SEASON

> A sluggard does not plow in *season;* so at harvest time he looks but
> finds nothing. (Proverbs 20:4)

Because there are particular seasons for different activities, it's important that we do things at the proper time. As the verse points out,
it's not only important *what* we do and *how* we do it, but *when* we do it is
also important. We can prepare the soil and plant corn seeds, but if we
do it in the middle of winter then we won't have as good a crop of corn
as we might have had if we'd planted it in the spring.

ANIMALS ACT ACCORDING TO THE SEASONS

> Even the stork in the sky knows her appointed *seasons,* and the
> dove, the swift and the thrush observe the time of their migra-
> tion. But my people do not know the requirements of the LORD
> (Jeremiah 8:7)

THE MOON AND SEASONS

Many older farmers and gardeners who I would consider "born-again"
do much of their planting based on the phases of the moon. They don't
claim to do this because of superstition, but say that they do it because
the Bible says the moon was created to mark times and seasons.

> The moon marks off the seasons, and the sun knows when to
> go down. (Psalms 104:19)

Recently I have tried to start doing this as well, because it sounds consistent with Scripture. Science also shows us that the gravitational pull of
the moon regulates the growth of plants. I use an almanac to determine
which dates would be best to plant. (Almanacs also tend to have supersti-
tious astrological things in them as well, but I try to ignore them.)

Even if there is no benefit to planting by the moon, I have benefited from
doing it because it gives me a schedule to go by. If I know that I need to
plant corn next Thursday or Friday, I am a lot more likely to get it done
than if I merely have a broad, two month window in which I need to do it.
Sometimes, as a farmer who works for myself, it's nice to have something
outside of myself to help regulate my work schedule. Since marking time
was part of the purpose of the moon, it works well.

God created the animals so they would base their activity around the seasons. This is something that the animals do and it would seem a wise thing for us to do. This also implies that it would be easiest to manage animals if we took into account the seasons.

THE PROVISION OF GOD COMES IN SEASON

Yet he has not left himself without testimony: He has shown kindness by giving you rain from heaven and crops in their seasons; he provides you with plenty of food and fills your hearts with joy." (Acts 14:17)

The eyes of all look to you, and you give them their food at the *proper time.* (Psalms 145:15)

One other thing I see in Scripture regarding seasons is that God promises to provide for us in the proper season. In the verses above we see that God gives us crops and food, not all the time, but in the proper time and appropriate season.

SEASONS IN CREATION

In creation the seasons come and go every year affecting and regulating the cycles of living things. Seasons differ from place to place; some places have four distinct seasons, while others have a rainy season and a dry one. However, we distinctly see the fact that life changes according to the seasons. During one season plants and animals thrive, and in another they are more dormant. Most plants grow in the summer. A few plants grow in the winter. Animals tend to have their young in the spring and summer. Seeds will wait until just the right time and then they sprout. The seasons are part of life on the earth and we observe that everything grows *best* in its proper season.

GROWING IN SEASON

We can honor the design of the seasons in our production methods by seeking to grow things and perform activities in the proper season. Not that it's a sin to try and grow tomatoes in the winter in a greenhouse, or breed your animals to give birth at any time other than springtime. However, we need to recognize the wisdom of God in the way He has established the seasons and the benefits that come from honoring that. Things grow better in the season that they were designed for. We may grow tomatoes in a greenhouse, but it's going to take a lot of work and probably not produce fruit as good as summer-grown tomatoes. It would be wise for us as farmers to try and honor the seasons as much as possible.

CHARACTERISTICS OF SEASONAL PRODUCTION

So what are some ways we can try to honor and grow according the seasons in our production methods?

PLANT AT THE PROPER SEASON

When we plant our gardens, we can honor the seasons by trying to plant each thing during the proper time for our area. I know this seems obvious, but I have been guilty of just going out and planting something without researching the proper season. Thankfully, today we have many resources that can give us good planting dates for our area. We should use them if we want to produce good fruit.

BREED IN SEASON

When we breed animals it would be good if we took into account our seasons and the time that animals in our area naturally breed. It can make it a lot easier if you don't have to care for young critters through the cold in some areas, or the heat in others. In places like Canada, with harsh winters, it would be more critical to breed at a certain time than where I live. Alabama weather is much milder and gives us more flexibility. We raise our meat chickens in the spring and fall when the days are cooler. The chickens can overheat in the summer, and their water will freeze in the winter. I also try to honor the seasons' effect on my laying hens. Many people put lights in their chickens coops at night in the winter time because of the shorter days. On shorter days fewer eggs are laid. I don't believe it's a sin to put a light in with your chickens. However, I have tried to honor the seasons and care for my chickens by allowing their egg production to change with the seasons.

I might make a little less money, but it's likely better for the chickens or God wouldn't have made them that way.

PRINCIPLE #3: INTENDED ROLES

God created plants and animals to perform certain roles in certain ways.

Let's say you went out in your backyard and built a decorative, lightweight trellis out of sticks for a flowering vine you planted. If one of your children comes out and starts climbing on it and using it as a playground, you would probably stop them. Why? Because you didn't design your trellis to be climbed and played on by children. You designed it to support a plant and be beautiful. Although it might work as a piece of playground equipment, it will work best if it's used for its intended role.

The same thing applies to the things God has designed. Our management of them is going to be most effective and fruitful if we give them the jobs they were created to do.

When God created the plants and the animals he designed them to do a certain job under certain conditions. The specifics of this job might vary as the creature adapts to its environment (natural selection, not evolution—see "God's Design and Natural Selection" on the following page) but as I said at the beginning of this chapter, living things are not just building blocks. They have been designed to fulfill a specific role and we need to honor that in the way we manage them.

ROLES AND SCRIPTURE

There are not many direct Scriptures about the importance of honoring the roles of living creatures. We do see in Scripture some chapters, like Job 39, in which there is a description of many different animals and the roles God gave them. We understand the principle of the roles of God's plants and animals primarily by studying God's creation. If God in His wisdom, created all things, including our livestock and crops, then we must honor the original roles God gave to them.

Roles and Creation

In creation we see that plants and animals thrive best in their intended relationships, jobs, and environment. It's interesting to me to see how well things thrive when they fulfill the purpose for which they were designed. Here in Alabama, when we clear land or disturb the soil, there are plants just itching to come in and fill that "job opening". Fast growing weeds race to cover the ground I cultivate in my garden in obedience to God's design that the "land produce vegetation". Shrubs and bushes spring up along the wood-line of our freshly cleared pasture to take advantage of the opportunities provided by the edge. Frogs and dragonflies quickly populated the small pond that we built, happily doing their jobs and making the land more productive. Each living thing thrives and does best at that which it was designed by God to do.

Characteristics of Roles

If plants and animals function best when they are fulfilling their intended role, how should that impact our production methods? What are some particular things we could do to apply the principle of roles?

1. UTILIZE GOD'S DESIGN CHARACTERISTICS IN THE WORK OF THE FARM

I believe that each plant and animal should be given work to do on the farm based on their observable roles and design characteristics. This will produce the best results with the least amount of effort. *The more we let creation do what God designed it to do, the less work we*

GOD'S DESIGN AND NATURAL SELECTION

When God designed His creation, He didn't limit it to staying the same. No. He was much more creative than that. He built into the design of His creatures the ability to adapt to changes in their environment. I am not talking about evolution— the increase of genetic information to produce new species. I am referring to the incredible genetic complexity and capability of creatures to express different traits based on the nature of their surroundings. It's awe-inspiring that God's creative designs have the ability to adapt to a certain extent.

have to do because we are working with creation instead of fighting against it. In order to let animals do the work they were designed to do, the first thing we need to do is observe and identify what they were designed for and what they are qualified to do, as if we were reading a résumé. Next, we need to look at how we can utilize those roles to accomplish work. Let's look at a few examples:

- Pigs root and wallow: We can use the rooting of the pig to turn compost and plow our garden. We can use the wallowing of the pigs to seal leaky ponds.

- Chickens scratch and peck and eat bugs. We can use the chicken's scratching and pecking to clean up our gardens, break down organic material for compost, and mow grass. We can use the chickens' bug eating to control parasites in the garden and pests in the orchard.

- Trees provide shade and leaves. We can use the tree's shade to protect animals, plants, or buildings from the heat and sun. We can use the tree's leaves as mulch or compost.

- Grass grows blades and roots and covers the ground. The grass blades can be used as feed. The tendency of the roots to spread and cover the ground can be used to prevent erosion and improve soil drainage.

2. FOCUS ON GROWING VARIETIES
AND BREEDS SUITABLE FOR YOUR REGION

If we take a plant that was intended to produce fruit in a hot climate, and place it in a cold climate, it will probably not produce fruit or it will require more work than it's worth to produce fruit. Therefore, it will be best if we observe what varieties of plants and animals grow well in our region and focus our production around those varieties. In the southern U.S., we have a temperate climate. Therefore, although we can grow tropical plants with protection (which we do), it would be best to focus the majority of our farm around the production of native things. In Alabama, that would be things like blueberries, blackberries, figs, and muscadine grapes. Although we do have a few lemon trees and an orange tree that we keep in the greenhouse through the winter, our main orchard consists of the native plants that require a whole lot less work because they are in their intended climate.

PRINCIPLE #4: REST PERIODS

The land isn't to be worked continuously because of our greed, but should rather have periods of rest.

Work has been around from the beginning of time. God worked for six days creating the universe and everything in it. He also gave man work to do even before the fall and curse. Part of man's work was to use God's world to create abundance.

In the beginning, in addition to instituting work, God set a pattern that work should not be done continuously. The work that we do should be broken up with regular periods of rest. Rest isn't just an inconvenient necessity that is the result of getting tired. God doesn't tire—yet He rested the seventh day after creating. Instead, it's a pattern by which we acknowledge our dependence upon the Lord.

REST AND SCRIPTURE

In Scripture there are many examples of rest. Let's look at a few of them.

> Remember the Sabbath day by keeping it holy. Six days you shall labor and do all your work, but the seventh day is a Sabbath to the LORD your God. On it *you shall not do any work*, neither you, nor your son or daughter, nor your manservant or maidservant, nor your animals, nor the alien within your gates. For in six days the LORD made the heavens and the earth, the sea, and all that is in them, but he rested on the seventh day. Therefore the LORD blessed the Sabbath day and made it holy. (Exodus 20:8–11)

We see that the pattern of resting every seventh day was established by God. It didn't just apply to people, but also to animals.

> But in the seventh year the *land* is to have a sabbath of *rest,* a sabbath to the LORD. Do not sow your fields or prune your vineyards. Do not reap what grows of itself or harvest the grapes of your untended vines. The *land* is to have a year of *rest.* (Leviticus 25:4–5)

Not only are we and our animals to rest, but the land is to rest. Continuous work isn't consistent with the way God set things up to work. If anything works, including animals or land, then it must rest.

> Six days do your work, but on the seventh day do not work, so that your ox and your donkey may *rest* and the slave born in your household, and the alien as well, may be *refreshed.* (Exodus 23:11–12)

One reason that God wants us to rest is so that we may be refreshed from the toil of our work. God doesn't need refreshing, He is the source of refreshing, but because we are fallible and affected by the curse of sin, we need times of rest for refreshing.

> Come to me, all you who are weary and burdened, and I [Jesus] will give you *rest.* (Matthew 11:28)

The source of true rest is the Lord Jesus Christ. We will never find true rest apart from Him. Hebrews 4 also speaks of the coming Sabbath Rest for God's people, when they will rest from all the toil of this life.

> Six days you shall labor, but on the seventh day you shall *rest;* even during the *plowing* season and *harvest* you must *rest.* (Exodus 34:21)

The principle of resting helps cultivate in our hearts a trust in the Lord and confidence in His provision. Sometimes we may be tempted to think that there are times we need to work and can't afford to rest. One of the reasons God wants us to rest is to be reminded that we are dependent on Him for provision, not on our own strength and ability to work.

REST AND CREATION

When we look at untended creation, it obviously doesn't rest from being worked by man because it hasn't been worked by man. I have observed in creation that few, if any, living creatures work all the time. Animals work during the day *or* during the night. Most plants grow during one part of the season, and seemingly rest during the other. We also see the detrimental effects of man overworking the land without rest: erosion, decrease in fertility, buildup of disease in the soil. All of these things are evidence that work without rest is not a good thing and not what God desires.

Rest Doesn't Mean Neglect

I should clarify what I believe Biblical rest means. The Bible clearly states rest means to stop work. We saw in the preceding passages that when God says to rest on the Sabbath, He goes on to explain that no work shall be done. However, what exactly does that look like? Does it mean that we shouldn't get out of bed on the Sabbath? Should we cook meals? Does it mean that we shouldn't feed our animals?

What is meant by *work?* Work is the application of energy and strength in utilizing available resources for the production of desired action or fruits. Work involves effort, and utilizes and escalates the productivity and fruitfulness of land, animals, and people. Rest, therefore, would mean ceasing from the increased effort and application of energy, keeping productivity at a sustainable level and allowing for the refreshing of everything that was working.

Rest gives us a time of refreshing from the toil of our work, but we should still care for the needs of our land, animals, and family.

We must realize that rest does not mean that we should cease from *all* effort or activity. If we stopped doing anything and just sat around, an extended period of rest would be detrimental to ourselves and to everything we are responsible for. God gave man the job of working and *caring* for the land. Therefore, I believe that we should rest and be refreshed while we continue to meet the needs of our family, our land, and our animals.

Rest means that we cease from working creation, but not from caring for it. Resting does not justify neglect.

When God created and rested on the seventh day He ceased from all the work He had done, but He obviously didn't cease from caring for and maintaining His creation. Without the care of God all of creation would fall apart. Through Him all things hold together (Colossians 1:17) and have their being (Revelation 4:11). Therefore, in following His example, we need to rest from work, but not neglect the care of what we are responsible for.

Christ rebuked the religious leaders of Israel when they tried to condemn His caring for and healing people on the Sabbath.

> Indignant because Jesus had healed on the Sabbath, the synagogue ruler said to the people, "There are six days for work. So come and be healed on those days, not on the Sabbath."
>
> The Lord answered him, "You hypocrites! Doesn't each of you on the Sabbath untie his ox or donkey from the stall and lead it out to give it water? (Luke 13:14–15)

CHARACTERISTICS OF REST

How can we begin to apply God's principle of rest to the way that we farm? Here are a few practical suggestions:

PROVIDE PERIODS OF REST FOR THE LAND

When we work our land we also need to let it rest. In our planning, we need to have times when our land has a break from the sowing and reaping we use to increase its productivity. This can mean that we let it lay "fallow" at least every seventh year. Another way would be to let at least a seventh of your land lay fallow every year. If you let it lay fallow, I don't believe this means you shouldn't care for it. Just because we don't work it doesn't mean that we should let it grow up with a crop of invasive weeds that spread noxious seeds all over the place. Mowing your land or even growing a green manure crop for the benefit of the soil during the fallow year could all be an application of caring for your soil while letting it rest. However, anything that takes from the soil or makes it exert energy, such as plowing and harvesting plants, would be working the land and probably wouldn't be considered "rest."

If you farm on a very small scale, it can seem more difficult to know how to apply the principle of rest. If you have only a window box or one raised bed, how do you let it rest? There is no single right answer and this principle is focused more on your heart than on your dirt. You might decide to put new soil in your pot every so often or you might grow a cover crop in your raised bed during part of the season. The primary objective is to express your heart's dependence on God while you guard against greed.

ALLOW FOR PERIODS OF REST FOR ANIMALS

In order to make sure our animals rest we need to identify the ways we work them. It's hard to tell whether just feeding our animals for meat would be considered work but it seems pretty clear that managing for increased production of products such as milk and eggs, or utilizing the strength of draft animals would be considered work. These are the things that we should let them rest from. And I don't mean we shouldn't milk our cow or collect eggs from our chickens on the Sabbath. That is part of caring for them. Trying to get the most milk for the longest period of time or trying to squeeze the greatest number of eggs out of our chickens by putting lights in their coop might be straying from the desire to give them rest. God gives us rest and we should desire to do the same with the animals He has given us to rule over.

REST ONE DAY IN SEVEN

If we want to know how often we should rest we have but to look at the example and commandment of God. In the Ten Commandments God commands that we should rest one day in seven because He Himself rested on the seventh day after His work of creating. As farmers, we should emulate that. God told the Israelites to rest on the Sabbath even during the busy seasons of plowing and harvest. We shouldn't plan as if we had seven days to work. We need to make sure that we work hard for six days so we won't need to work on the seventh. Finally, we need to trust that God will provide what we need from the faithful work of six days a week.

CONCLUSION

If we want our farms to be successful we need to seek to honor the principles of God's design as seen in Scripture and creation. This chapter looked at four general principles:

- Healthy soil results in healthy plants.

- The changing seasons affect plants and animals.

- God created plants and animals to function in certain ways, filling certain roles on the farm.

- God commands us to make time for rest.

These are not the only principles that we can observe and implement, but they can be a useful starter. God is the all-wise Creator, and the closer we can copy and utilize His wisdom the more sustainable and fruitful our farms will be.

7

PATTERNS IN GOD'S DESIGN

How can we honor the patterns God put in creation?

To develop Christian farming methods, we need to not only seek to apply some of the principles we see in Scripture and creation, but I believe we should also seek to copy some of the natural patterns and designs we see in creation.

PATTERNS FOR PLANT PRODUCTION

What are some of God's patterns we could copy in growing plants? These include *mulch, proper tillage,* and *diversity.*

Mulch

In creation, whenever we see plants growing, we almost always see the ground covered with some kind of mulch. Mulch is loose material, normally dead plant matter. Christian farming pioneer Brian Oldreive of Foundations for Farming calls mulch "God's Blanket". If you go into a forest, you will see the ground covered by a mulch of leaves. If you go out into a meadow you will find the ground covered with a blanket of dead and living grasses. There are many benefits that mulch provides to the soil and plants:

- Protects the surface of the ground from compaction by rain or treading. Allows plants to sprout and take root.

- Keeps the soil moist through decreasing loss of water by evaporation. Plants can thrive better in dry seasons.

- Reduces loss of soil through erosion by slowing water and allowing it to soak in.

- Decomposing mulch builds soil and promotes microorganisms. Plants are provided with a steady supply of diverse nutrients.

- Mulch prevents soil from splattering up on plants and reduces the risk of soil-borne diseases.

- Heavy mulches eliminate the sprouting of new weeds.

Rarely in God's creation will you ever find bare soil except where man has removed the covering of mulch. To me this indicates that mulching is a design God intended for the health of soil and plants and would therefore be beneficial for us to copy in our production methods. On my farm, I have found heavy mulches to be very beneficial in small, intensive areas and gardens. However, on a larger scale, heavy mulches are more difficult to apply and I have ended up using lighter mulches and shallow cultivation for weeds.

PROPER TILLAGE

There are many prominent Christian farmers today who are promoting no-till farming as a good way to honor God's design in soil management and crop production. I agree with what they say and am trying to learn to implement some of their methods. However, even though I believe that no-till is a great idea, I still believe that plowing, or tilling, can be done in a way that is consistent with His design as well. We do see minimal soil disturbance in creation, but we also see pigs that root up the soil, and birds that scratch back the mulch. In Scripture we also see in multiple places references to plowing, including the following passage:

Listen and hear my voice; pay attention and hear what I say. When a farmer *plows* for planting, does he plow continually? Does he keep on breaking up and *harrowing* the soil? When he has leveled the surface, does he not sow caraway and scatter cummin? Does he not plant wheat in its place, barley in its plot, and spelt in its field? *His God instructs him and teaches him the right way.* (Isaiah 28:23–26)

This passage not only talks about plowing and harrowing, but also indicates that there is a *right* way to go about them. What would be the proper way to plow and harrow? First we must realize what Scripture is referring to when it talks about plowing. It's not talking about breaking and turning the soil with a steel, John Deere moldboard plow. The plows that they used were probably more like chisel plows. When Isaiah 2:4 speaks about beating swords into plowshares, it seems to indicate more of a pointed, chisel-type plow than a turning-type plow. With that in mind, let's consider some possible principles that could define "proper tillage" methods.

- PROPER TILLAGE *WOULD*
  open up the soil for drainage
  break up the soil for good germination

- PROPER TILLAGE WOULD *NOT*
  frequently mix up the layers of the soil, destroying soil life and incorporating mulch into the soil.

The use of a chisel-type plow and harrow would be consistent with these principles. The chisel plow would open up the soil for drainage without mixing up the layers too much, and the harrow would break up the soil for good germination without incorporating the mulch too deep in the ground.

The frequent use of the moldboard plow or deep rotary tiller, on the other hand, does not seem to be consistent with proper tillage principles. They both mix the layers of the soil and incorporate the mulch into the soil, while failing to effectively open the soil below for drainage.

On my farm I have gone from the moldboard plow and deep tilling to minimal chisel plowing and shallow tilling. The latter has done much to improve the structure and worm population of my soil.

However, especially when on an increased scale of production, there are times when a moldboard plow or rotary tiller is useful for turning under sod for a new garden when I don't have time for using chickens to eat it down. It is hard to come up with a helpful formula for proper tillage that applies universally. Each region varies in soil type, rainfall, temperature, and sunlight, and it requires experience and wisdom to know how to best steward your soil.

DIVERSITY

Another pattern for plant growth we see in creation is that of diversity. Rarely do we see only one variety of plant growing in one place. Normally plants grow among a diverse system of other plants and animals which benefit each other. There are many benefits of growing a diversity of plants rather than a large concentration of one type.

DISTINCTION OF KINDS

In the Old Testament (Lev. 19:19, Deut. 22:2) we read that God told the Israelites to not plant "mingled seed." There is controversy among many over exactly what that means. Some would argue that this implies monoculture. Others would say it means to not hybridize. I don't claim to have the answer, but I believe the general principle that we should apply is that of honoring the distinction of the different kinds that God created, not just trying to have separate fields for everything we plant. Also, the fact that planting two things in a vineyard defiled it seems to indicate to me that the specific application of this commandment was ceremonial in nature. In Chapter Eight I will discuss some particular application today for this principle.

- The diversity of plants allows for more productivity per acre than a monoculture. If you plant apple trees at sixty percent normal density per acre and blackberries between them at sixty percent density as well, then you are producing twenty percent more per acre than you would have if you had planted only one thing.

- A diversity of plants is less susceptible to bugs and pests. In creation, the reason we seldom see a monoculture is because too much of one plant in an area attracts "pests" who are just doing their job of bringing things back into balance.

- A diversity of plants is less likely to have a total failure in one year. This is the idea of "casting your bread upon the waters", or of "not putting all your eggs in one basket". If frost gets all the fruit trees one year, then your vegetables will still be there. If blight gets all of your tomatoes, then you still have your corn and squash.

In my garden I have tried to apply the pattern of biodiversity by breaking up my plantings into numerous smaller plantings. Instead of planting all my tomato plants in one spot, I plant them in two, three, or more spots throughout the garden. Disease and bugs can't leap from plant to plant and ruin the whole crop. Instead, they leap from tomato plant to tomato plant and then run into a squash plant and stop. Planting them in different spots has also helped in case one area of the garden floods or is too dry.

When seeking to increase diversity in our plant production it's important to take into consideration the relationships of the plants. Some plants benefit each other when in close proximity, and others harm each other. We need to place plants where they will do the most good. For example, if we plant a garden and place something tall like corn where it prevents the sun from reaching other, smaller, sun-loving plants, then it could cause the growth of the smaller plants to be stunted. If, instead, we placed the corn where it acted as a windbreak and shelter for the small plants, then it could actually promote their growth. Or, if it were shading some lettuces, it could keep them from getting bitter from the heat. Other plants do well together because they have different root systems (shallow and deep) or require different nutrients.

PATTERNS FOR ANIMAL PRODUCTION

Let's take a look at a few of God's patterns in creation that might be useful in raising animals. This isn't exhaustive, but it could get you started in looking for and copying other patterns. We'll look at *rotational foraging, natural habitats,* and *natural diets.*

Rotational Foraging

Grazing animals such as cattle, sheep, horses and foraging animals like chickens and pigs use a pattern of rotational foraging. In the wild, we see that animals who forage are always moving. Birds don't scratch in the same spot every day. Herds of buffalo don't graze the same area each week. They keep moving to fresh areas of forage. This gives the land that is grazed time to rest and produce more forage. The concept of moving animals from place to place is mentioned in Scripture:

> People will live together in Judah and all its towns—farmers and those who move about with their flocks. (Jeremiah 31:24)

Our production methods should try to copy this pattern if we want to be successful. This isn't an area of obedience or disobedience, but just sound advice consistent with the design of God. There are many being promoted that already apply this pattern. Joel Salatin and others have pioneered a return to rotational foraging.

WILD ANIMALS AND LIVESTOCK
Just recently I noticed that in the beginning God created, not just animals, but wild animals and livestock. Up until that time I had always pictured all livestock as domesticated wild animals (which some are). But this thinking is the result of evolutionary influence. God created some animals to primarily be the servants of men from the very beginning!

In general, the pattern of rotational foraging means that we should try to move foraging animals around so they don't stay in the same spot for too long. Here are a few examples of applications:

- Grazing animals are frequently moved to small paddocks instead of leaving them to range in one big field. Animals are limited to what is in their small paddock and eat everything more completely, even weeds they would normally ignore. (When left to roam, they tend to graze out the good grasses and plants and leave the weeds, creating poor pastures.) The pasture gets a longer period of rest between grazings.

- Move chickens around in portable coops or shelters. This keeps them from killing the grass (unless you want it killed because it's in your garden) and keeps the application of manure at a rate the soil can handle. It also breaks up the life-cycle of parasites that build up and reproduce in the soil.

NATURAL HABITAT

Another pattern that would be useful to follow in the production of animals is that of their natural habitat. In creation we can see that every animal has a specific habitat or environment in which it was intended to live and function. Obviously, fish were intended to live in a wet environment, and worms were intended to live in the ground. If these creatures are placed in an environment other than the one for which they were designed, we can't expect them to function well. In our methods of raising animals we should seek to place them in an environment comparable to their intended habitat.

Let's look at a few practical examples:

- Chickens are birds and their natural habitat is generally outdoors in woodland and meadow. It would make sense to raise them outdoors in forest or pasture! Sadly, most chickens raised today are in buildings where they hardly ever see the sun. It's not a sin to keep a chicken in a barn at some point, but if God designed them to live outdoors, then we need to recognize that that would probably be the best place to raise them. Methods that allow chickens to be outdoors to forage on the ground would be the most

If these creatures are placed in an environment other than the one for which they were designed, then we can't expect them to function well.

consistent with honoring the habitat God intended for them.

- Pigs' natural habitat is also woodland and meadow. The best way to raise pigs, therefore, would be to allow pigs to be outside in the woodlands and meadows. Sadly, most of today's pigs are raised inside.

- Cows were designed to live primarily in pasture/meadow. We should probably raise them in a pasture, not in a feedlot devoid of grass, standing in their own manure.

Natural Diet

If we want to follow God's patterns and design in raising animals, then we need to try to feed them what they were intended to eat. This may seem obvious, but this principle is violated in many areas of animal husbandry today. For example, most cows today, who have stomachs perfectly designed for primarily a grass diet, are fed corn. Worse than that, I have a brochure from our state extension service detailing the benefits of feeding chicken manure to beef cattle. If the way God designed things to work was "good," then violating His design and doing something like feeding cows chicken manure is obviously not good!

In order to honor the natural diet of each animal we need to determine what their natural diet is. Then we can find ways to provide a natural diet for our animals. We don't just want something that "works." We want to feed our animals in a way that glorifies God's design.

With my chickens I have observed and read that they naturally eat grains, bugs and meat, grit and minerals, and grass and greens. I have tried to make those things available for them as much as possible. The better job I do of providing them the food they need, the healthier the chickens are and the better eggs they produce.

As we observe and honor the patterns God has placed in creation, we will increase the ways our farms bring glory to Him.

CONCLUSION

I look forward to seeing the Christian farming methods that will be developed as born-again farmers begin to get serious about farming for the glory of God. The patterns reviewed in this chapter are by no means the only ones, and they aren't guarantees of success by themselves. But by studying and observing the patterns in creation, we can gain incredible insight into the amazing wisdom of God.

8

GROWING FRUIT FOR THE TEMPLE

What does God want us to grow?

The purpose of what we grow is to provide for the physical needs of people in a way that honors the design and intent of God.

AS CHRISTIAN FARMERS WE NEED TO make sure that what we are growing honors the Lord. We need to be producing things that fulfill the purposes of our farming. Since our lives and our land belong to God, we need to make sure we are using them to produce fruit that honors Him.

Farmer Brian Oldreive once managed one of the largest tobacco farms in Africa. After becoming a born-again Christian, he continued to grow tobacco until one night he read 1 Corinthians 10:31: "So whether you eat or drink or whatever you do, do it all for the glory of God." He was cut to the heart and vowed to never grow another leaf of tobacco because he was convicted that he was growing poison for thousands of people. As a result of trying to switch to other crops, Mr. Oldreive lost everything he owned. But, because of his faithfulness and obedience, God eventually blessed him with farming wisdom that has helped thousands of poor farmers in Africa through his Foundations for Farming ministry.[1]

---

1   http://www.foundationsforfarming.org/

WHAT'S THE PURPOSE OF WHAT WE PRODUCE?

The purpose of what we grow is to *provide for the physical needs of people in a way that honors the design and intent of God.* For those of us who are born-again, this is important because we are providing for the needs of the temple of the Holy Spirit, who lives inside us. Of course there are many things that we grow to meet the needs of our livestock, but if we are talking about the final end product, then the purpose is to meet the needs of people. The greatest commandment is to love our neighbor. What we grow should promote and benefit those who use and consume it.

WHAT ARE THE NEEDS OF OUR NEIGHBORS?

God doesn't need anything, but He created man with needs that could only be met by God. God primarily provides for these needs through the fruit of the soil.

> But if we have *food* and *clothing*, we will be content with that. (1 Timothy 6:8)

> Suppose a brother or sister is without *clothes* and *daily food*. If one of you says to him, "Go, I wish you well; keep warm and well fed," but does nothing about his *physical needs*, what good is it? (James 2:15–16)

The most basic physical needs of man are food and clothing. In order to survive and thrive, we have got to have something to eat and something to wear. If the primary purpose of our agriculture is to provide for the needs of ourselves and others, then it appears that we need to be growing things that are either good to eat or useful for making clothes and building homes.

WHAT HAS GOD PROVIDED FOR OUR NEEDS?

You have your farm or yard or window box. You want to be a good steward and make it beautiful, fruitful, and easily managed. You know you want to grow stuff that will help provide for the needs of you, your family, and maybe your neighbors. So what should you be growing to help fill those needs?

Take a look at the things God has made available to us. He has promised to meet our every need. We need to look and see how God is meeting our needs.

The major products we can grow and produce on our farms fall under two categories, *food* and *fiber*. These two categories supply the basic needs. The food category obviously includes things we can eat like fruits, vegetables, grains, dairy, eggs, and meat. The fiber category includes things that provide materials for producing clothing and for building shelter, things like cotton, flax, wool, silk, and wood.

WHAT DOES GOD WANT US TO GROW FOR FOOD?

Food is the primary product of most farms. We see this referred to in Psalm 104:14–15:

> He makes grass grow for the cattle, and plants for man to *culti-vate*—bringing forth *food* from the earth: *wine* that gladdens the heart of man, *oil* to make his face shine, and *bread* that sustains his heart.

This verse talks about plants as food. Does that mean we should only grow plants for food? Is it wrong to eat animals? Or should we only raise and eat clean animals like sheep and cattle? Does that mean no pigs? This is a big topic (and quite controversial), but let's think about what would be *best* to grow for food. The Bible tells us about what God intends for us to eat. Here is a list of the changes I see to what is acceptable to eat:

1. AT FIRST, ONLY SEED-BEARING PLANTS WERE GIVEN AS FOOD

Then God said, "I give you every seed-bearing plant on the face of the whole earth and every tree that has fruit with seed in it. They will be yours for food. (Genesis 1:29)

2. MEAT WAS GIVEN AS FOOD AFTER THE FLOOD

Everything that lives and moves will be food for you. Just as I gave you the green plants, I now give you everything. (Genesis 9:3)

3. CERTAIN MEATS WERE UNCLEAN UNDER CEREMONIAL LAW

You must distinguish between the unclean and the clean, between living creatures that may be eaten and those that may not be eaten. (Leviticus 11:47)

4. ALL FOODS PERMISSIBLE UNDER COVENANT OF GRACE

Then a voice told him, "Get up, Peter. Kill and eat." "Surely not, Lord!" Peter replied. "I have never eaten anything impure or unclean." The voice spoke to him a second time, "Do not call anything impure that God has made clean." (Acts 10:13–15)

Summed up, the journey of acceptable food throughout history has been seed-bearing plants and no meat, then meat, then only clean meat, then all food was declared clean.

Since we are saved by the grace of Christ, I believe there are no longer any binding commands about specific animals we can't eat.

> For the Kingdom of God is not a matter of eating and drinking, but of righteousness, peace and joy in the Holy Spirit, because anyone who serves Christ in this way is pleasing to God and approved by men. (Romans 14:17–18)

But we can't just plant whatever we want because we have a responsibility to show love to those for whom we grow food. And just because all food is fine for consumption, doesn't mean it's *best*. Though the ceremonially clean foods are no longer required, there are still many health benefits from them. (I realize that there are many different views concerning the applicability of Biblical dietary laws and do not claim to be smarter than those holding a different view. All I attempt to do here is simply state what I feel the Scriptures teach at this point in my life. May we not "destroy the work of God for the sake of food" [Romans 14:20].)

Thankfully, the Lord gives us some clarity concerning the freedom we have in Christ regarding food. The following passage is from 1 Corinthians 10:23–26:

> "Everything is permissible"—but not everything is beneficial. "Everything is permissible"—but not everything is constructive. Nobody should seek his own good, but the good of others. Eat anything sold in the meat market without raising questions of conscience, for, "The earth is the Lord's, and everything in it."

This passage is telling us that the food that we eat and grow is no longer just a matter of *do*s and *don't*s. It's a matter of the heart. The food that we eat and the food that we grow should spring forth from a heart that seeks the good of others. It's a selfish farmer who goes about his work concerned only with what is permissible, rather than seeking to produce what is beneficial. *As Christian farmers we should be seeking to produce and provide the highest quality food possible.*

This not only means trying to grow varieties of plants and animals that are good for food, but seeking to be faithful stewards in the way we produce them, primarily by enriching the soil. Remember, healthy soil equals healthy plants.

SO WHAT IS QUALITY FOOD?

We are asking not just what type of food is okay to eat, but what defines the best type of food according to God's definition of success?

Fundamentally, quality food provides a high degree of benefit to those who eat it. This benefit isn't simply in terms of enjoyment, but in promoting general health and well being. For food to do that, it needs to be not only safe to eat, but highly nutritious as well.

All food isn't created equal. In our culture today we view food as a commodity. Corn is just corn. Beef is just beef. An egg is just an egg. But that's not true. The way something is produced and the variety that is grown has a significant effect on the nutritional quality of food.

Effects of Production on Nutrition

Studies support the idea that there is nutritional advantage in crops, eggs, milk, and meat that have been produced using more natural techniques rather than using conventional techniques that violate the basic principles and patterns of God's creation.

- HEALTHIER EGGS

  For example, a study was done that tested the nutritional value of eggs from over a dozen farms that keep their laying chickens on pasture so they can forage and eat grass. Compared to conventional, factory-farm raised eggs, the eggs from pastured hens contained:

  - $\frac{1}{3}$ less cholesterol than commercial eggs

  - $\frac{1}{4}$ less saturated fat

  - $\frac{2}{3}$ more vitamin A

  - 2 times more omega-3 fatty acids

  - 7 times more beta carotene[2]

- BETTER BEEF

  Another study claimed that cows that are fed grass, as God designed them to eat, are superior nutritionally to grain-fed cows:

  > Growing consumer interest in grass-fed beef products has raised a number of questions with regard to the perceived differences in nutritional quality between grass-fed and grain-fed cattle. Research spanning three decades suggests that grass-based diets can significantly improve the fatty acid (FA) composition

---

2   Cheryl Long and Tabitha Alterman, "Meet Real Free-Range Eggs," *Mother Earth News,* October/November 2007, http://www.motherearthnews.com/Real-Food/2007-10-01/Tests-Reveal-Healthier-Eggs.aspx.

and antioxidant content of beef, albeit with variable impacts on overall palatability. Grass-based diets have been shown to enhance total conjugated linoleic acid (CLA) (C18:2) isomers, trans vaccenic acid (TVA) (C18:1 t11), a precursor to CLA, and omega-3 (n-3) FAs on a g/g fat basis.[3]

- SUPERIOR MILK

  Another study claimed that naturally produced milk is nutritionally superior to conventional milk.[4]

The previous studies are just a few examples of how the diet and the way animals are raised affects the nutritional quality of food. The same thing applies to soil and plants. If we are merely trying to increase plant yields with chemical fertilizers and don't build the soil, then we may grow a lot of food, but it won't be very high in nutrients. Since the beginning of the use of chemical fertilizers and other improper soil management techniques we have seen a decrease in the nutritional quality of fruits and vegetables grown.[5] To add to this problem, the most commonly used herbicide today, Roundup, kills plants not by poisoning them, but by tying up the nutrients needed for them to survive. Plants that are Roundup resistant may survive, but they don't take up as many nutrients as they would otherwise.[6]

---

3   Daley et al.: A review of fatty acid profiles and antioxidant content in grass-fed and grain-fed beef. *Nutrition Journal* 2010 9:10.

4   Spiegel, Jan Ellen, "Organic Milk Beats Conventional Milk for Nutrition, Says UK Study," Slashfood, January 19, 2011, http://www.slashfood.com/2011/01/19/organic-milk-beats-conventional-milk-for-nutrition-says-uk-stud/.

5   Worthington, Virginia, "Nutritional Quality of Organic Versus Conventional Fruits, Vegetables, and Grains," *The Journal of Alternative and Complementary Medicine* 7, no. 2 (2001), 161-173, http://www.chiro.org/nutrition/FULL/Nutritional_Quality_of_Organic_Versus_Conventional_Fruits.html.

6   Smith, Jeffrey, "Monsanto's Roundup Triggers Over 40 Plant Diseases and Endangers Human and Animal Health," Institute for Responsible Technology, www.responsibletechnology.org/blog/664.

EFFECTS OF PLANT BREEDING ON NUTRITION

The goal of most breeding done today is to create plants that have longer shelf life, uniformity, more yield, and disease resistance. Research done by Biochemist Dr. Donald Davis in Texas suggests that the nutrient value of basic garden crops has declined in the past 50 years. Though part of this could be attributed to soil health, part of it is most likely due to plant breeding. Here is a quote from Dr. Davis:

> "We conclude that the most likely explanation [to diminishing nutritional value] was changes in cultivated varieties used today compared to 50 years ago." . . . "During those 50 years, there have been intensive efforts to breed new varieties that have greater yield, or resistance to pests, or adaptability to different climates. But the dominant effort is for higher yields. Emerging evidence suggests that when you select for yield, crops grow bigger and faster, but they don't necessarily have the ability to make or uptake nutrients at the same, faster rate."[7]

Other research claims that cornmeal from older varieties of corn has higher nutritional value than cornmeal from conventional corn.[8]

GROWING FOR NUTRITIONAL QUALITY

Here are a couple of suggestions of things we can do to grow the best quality, most nutritious food:

- *Make sure our production is based on healthy soil.* Hopefully you understand that if we want to have healthy plants and healthy food we need to have healthy soil. If the nutrition isn't in the soil, it's not going to be in the plants. In addition to manures and organic matter, some played-out soils may need actual mineral soil amendments like

---

7 "Study suggests nutrient decline in garden crops over past 50 years," The University of Texas at Austin, December 1, 2004, http://www.utexas.edu/news/2004/12/01/nr_chemistry/.

8 "The Declining Nutrient Value of Food," *Mother Earth News*, December 2011/January 2012, http://www.motherearthnews.com/sustainable-farming/nutrient-value-of-food-zmoz11zphe. aspx.

greensand applied to boost micronutrient levels in the soil. Increased earthworm population in the soils also help to bring up nutrients from the subsoil.

- *Grow older, less conventional varieties.* Some newer, higher yielding varieties of plants (and perhaps animals?) aren't as nutrient dense as older varieties. The newer varieties may grow twice as big, but still take up the same amount of nutrients, requiring you to eat twice as much for the same nutritional value. Sticking with heirloom or open-pollinated plants might be wise, especially because you can control breeding and seed production if desired.

- *Focus on Growing Clean Animals.* Although no longer required under the law of grace, the ceremonial restrictions still have many health benefits. For instance, many of the "unclean" animals are scavengers and predators, those most likely to be carrying a disease of some sort. Pigs carry tapeworms, which can spread to humans through pork if not cooked properly. That being said, I still eat bacon (and we are raising some pigs), but the majority of the meat we eat is "clean": beef, chicken, venison, and scaled fish. There appears to be wisdom in the ceremonially clean foods even today, so it would make sense to major on producing "clean" animals for food, and minor in the unclean animals like pigs.

WHY IS IT IMPORTANT TO GROW QUALITY FOOD?

The quality of the food we eat is a major factor in the health of our bodies.

Our bodies are designed by God to need certain nutrients and minerals that we get from food in order to function and stay healthy. A healthy body can fight off disease and sickness. But when our bodies don't have the proper nutrients (major-nutrients and micronutrients), they lack the proper fuel to run smoothly and they start falling apart. Here is a quote from a nutritional website:

> Insufficient micronutrient intake has short–term and long–term implications for disease risk. As an example, immune function is adversely affected by poor intakes of nearly every essential vitamin and mineral. Thus, diets lacking essential micronutrients may theoretically, at least, affect health over the short term by impairing resistance to viral or bacterial infection. Among longer term problems, a lack of nutrients required for DNA methylation and gene stability may increase the risk for certain cancers.[9]

Our bodies are truly amazing in what they can put up with. It's a miracle that we can feed our bodies personal-sized, processed snack cakes and a diet soda for lunch, and not die before supper! If we treated our cars like we treat our bodies, and put crude oil in the engine, and kerosene in the tank, it would destroy our vehicles.

The standard that most farmers shoot for in terms of our food quality is safety. We'd hate to think that we were making anyone sick. Hopefully no Christian farmer is going to spray his crops with anything that is known to harm people. However, just because an ear of corn we grow isn't bad for us, that doesn't mean it's particularly good either!

If we as farmers want to promote health and the general well-being of the people we serve with the things we produce as farmers, it's very important that we seek to grow food that's not only safe, but also full of nutrition! It takes more effort to improve our soils and use more traditional seed varieties, but what would we want someone to do for us? More importantly, what does God want us to do for others? We need to reflect God's love and care in the very nature of the food we grow.

HOW CAN WE HONOR THE DESIGN OF LIFE?

One of the hot topics today is genetic engineering. Genetically modified organisms (GMO's) are plants and animals that have been altered genetically in order to produce a trait that they wouldn't naturally

9　"Micronutrients in Health and Disease," NutrionMD.com, accessed February 8, 2012, http://www.nutritionmd.org/health_care_providers/general_nutrition/micronutrients.html.

have. GMO's are used extensively in agriculture today. Examples are the "Roundup Ready" varieties of corn, soybeans, cotton, etc., that are unaffected by the application of that herbicide.

At first glance genetic engineering sounds useful. But our question as Christian farmers is not "Do GMOs work?" but "Do they honor God?"

The way genetic engineering changes the characteristics of various plants and animals isn't the same as traditional breeding. Traditional breeding uses the selection of specific traits within a species. If you have a herd of dairy cows and want to improve their genetic expression so they can produce more milk, then you only select the offspring from the cows that produce the most milk. If you are growing tomatoes and want to have a variety that tastes better, then you only save seeds from the best-tasting tomatoes. This is merely a way of managing the natural, God-given adaptability of animals and plants.

Genetic engineering is different in that it involves taking the DNA from one species, say a fish, and inserting it into the DNA of a different species, say a tomato, in order to produce traits that you couldn't get through natural breeding. Today genetic engineering is used to produce organisms that are resistant to herbicides, or that produce more yields. Some GMOs even manufacture pharmaceuticals and drugs!

But our question as Christian farmers is not "Do GMOs work?" but "Do they honor God?"

In my opinion, the unnatural manipulation of genes violates the natural order of God's creation. When God created the plants and animals, anything that reproduces, He specifically distinguished them by *kinds*. He didn't just create "animals" and "plants" in general. He created different and distinct kinds of animals and plants. Look at how the the following verses demonstrate the emphasis placed on the fact that God created everything "according to its kind":

> Then God said, "Let the land produce vegetation: seed-bearing plants and trees on the land that bear fruit with seed in it, *according to their various kinds*." And it was so. (Genesis 1:11)

> So God created the great creatures of the sea and every living and moving thing with which the water teems, *according to their kinds,* and every winged bird *according to its kind.* And God saw that it was good. (Genesis 1:21)

> God made the wild animals *according to their kinds,* the livestock *according to their kinds,* and all the creatures that move along the ground *according to their kinds.* And God saw that it was good. (Genesis 1:25)

Another verse that speaks to the importance of honoring the distinction of the kinds (or species) that God created is found in Leviticus 19:19:

> Keep my decrees. Do not mate different *kinds* of animals. Do not plant your field with two *kinds* of seed. Do not wear clothing woven of two *kinds* of material.

These commands were originally given to Israel to help represent the separateness and holiness of God's people, but I also believe the principle behind this verse is specifically communicating the fact that we shouldn't mix kinds and species that don't naturally mix! If this is true, then we shouldn't be unnaturally mixing the DNA of different species. To do so is like saying that the way God designed creation isn't good enough and we need to improve it beyond the natural means He provided. Some also believe not mixing kinds means that even hybrids don't honor God's created order because they don't produce offspring that is true to its kind (or, sometimes, no offspring at all).

According to the Biblical definition of kinds are there different kinds of tomatoes? Or dogs? Kinds obviously refers to the distinction between a dog and a cat, a cow and a snake, and a fish and a tomato. But the fact that God said that there were different kinds of birds implies that it might mean more than that.

Much more could be said and debated about this topic. Perhaps we can all agree that if we acknowledge that God's ways are best, we should stick with the original varieties of fruits that He created and seek to avoid ones unnaturally tampered with by man. However, let's not get caught up in legalism and miss the principle. Just because you use GMOs doesn't mean that you are sinning, and just because you don't use them doesn't mean your heart is honoring to the Lord. The goal is to have a proper perspective on what pleases the Lord, and to pursue it wherever we are with whatever we have been given. I still have to use GMO grains in my chicken feed because I haven't developed a practical alternative in my area yet. I know that God will hold me accountable according to what He has given me and I know that He will help me make progress in my journey of seeking to honor Him in everything I do, even in the DNA of my chicken feed.

CONCLUSION

My desire isn't that you just take what I say about what God desires for us to grow as farmers and agree or disagree with it. I want you to begin to go to Lord and to His Word and ask Him to give you wisdom so you can find out what pleases Him. This is our great privilege as His children!

God has entrusted His land to us farmers to produce fruit, not in our own strength, of course, but through obedience and faithfulness. The quality of fruits that a farmer produces is an indication of whether he is a good farmer or not.

9

THE MINISTRY OF MARKETING

What does God want us to do with everything we grow?

FOR MANY OF US WHO LOVE FARMING, WE LOVE TO BE OUT WORKING the land. We enthusiastically prepare the ground in the spring, plant our crops, and tend them with care in hopeful anticipation of a bountiful harvest. However, when that harvest comes, many of us look at all the fruits and ask, "Now what?"

Marketing is an important aspect of farming that we as farmers often overlook or do poorly. If we don't have a good marketing plan then we will end up wasting much of what we grow. You can do a good job growing a successful crop, but if no one wants to buy it at harvest time you will still end up losing money.

In this chapter we will look at marketing and ask what God wants us to do with what we grow. Does He want us to sell it wholesale? Retail? Give it away? Who should we be marketing to? Should we eat some of what we produce ourselves?

From our perspective as stewards, we Christian farmers realize that the fruit we produce doesn't belong to us. We can't even claim ownership by thinking, "I grew this!" Alone, we can't grow anything. Everything that grows is a result of God's power and abundance.

MARKETING AS MINISTRY, NOT MANIPULATION

The goal of Biblical marketing is to allow us to best serve and provide for the needs of others. This is an application of the commandment to love your neighbor. Marketing involves communicating with and offering the things we grow to those who would benefit from them. Marketing is a form of ministering to the needs of others.

Instead of being about ministry, much of marketing today is about manipulation. The bottom line is simply to get someone to buy something—and this type of marketing can be very successful. It's successful at getting people to buy that new car they can't afford and don't need, or providing a credit card in hopes that the cardholder won't be faithful to pay it off so the credit card company can earn interest.

Many modern marketers don't care whether the people they're pitching to *need* what is being offered or not. Advertising is designed to create discontent and appeal to the fleshly desires of people. Ads make deceptive claims about products and services in order to entice buyers. We need to realize that these forms of marketing violate God's command to consider others' interests ahead of our own. We must guard against adopting manipulative strategies just because they are effective.

If we desire to serve those who buy what we produce, do we really want someone to buy something they don't need? I love selling the things we produce on our farm, and I can do a good job of it because I passionately believe that our products are beneficial to people's health. If I believe that I am offering something that is good for you, then I feel like I am doing you a service if I educate you and you become a customer as a result. However, I couldn't do that as well with things that are more of a luxury. I once considered doing blacksmithing for a living, but decided against it because the only way to make money blacksmithing today is to make unique metal art for wealthy people. I am not against providing people with more than the daily necessities, but if there's not a

Marketing is a form of ministering to the needs of others.

demand for my products, I have a hard time believing that God wants me to convince people to buy something they don't really need.

Marketing should be less about convincing people and more about educating people about their needs and letting them know what you have to offer. It should be less about manipulating their desires and more about ministering to their needs.

WHO SHOULD I PROVIDE FOR WITH THE FRUITS OF MY FARM?

Let's say we have grown some quality veggies or meats and want to use them to serve others. The problem now is, who of the billions of people in the world should you provide them to? Whoever will pay you the most or whoever agrees to buy the most? Thankfully, the Scriptures provide some clarity regarding whom we have a responsibility to serve.

1. OUR FIRST PRIORITY IS TO PROVIDE FOR OURSELVES AND OUR FAMILIES

As farmers, our first responsibility is to provide for our own needs and the needs of our family. If we are growing food and only have a little, then it should go to feed our household. This is the case for most gardeners. Feeding our families is a way we can provide directly for them, without having to sell what we grow. Most farmers sell everything they produce to those outside their household and then buy food. I would encourage farmers to begin to grow the actual food that their families eat. If you are trying to grow healthy food, doesn't it make sense that your family should get a share (1 Corinthians 9:7–10)? It's tempting for me to sell all I produce and buy the cheaper, less quality food at the store, but that would be neglecting my responsibility to my family and my own body.

It may sound selfish saying that our first responsibility is to provide for ourselves. But if we don't, then someone else has to.

> We hear that some among you are idle. They are not busy; they are busybodies. Such people we command and urge in the Lord Jesus

Christ to settle down and *earn the bread they eat.* (Thessalonians 3:11–12)

Our responsibility to provide for the needs of our family is seen in the following well known verse from 1 Timothy 5:8:

If anyone does not *provide* for his *relatives,* and especially for his immediate *family,* he has denied the faith and is worse than an unbeliever.

2. Our Second Priority is to Provide for our Brothers in Christ and our Neighbors

What if the Lord blesses us with more fruits than can be consumed by our own household? We should make it available for sale to those who are part of the church and those whom God has given us as neighbors. "Each of you should look not only to your own interests, but also to the interests of others" (Philippians 2:4). This is part of our duty to show love by seeking to meet the needs of others.

OUR BROTHERS IN CHRIST

By this all men will know that you are my disciples, if you love one another. (John 13:35)

In this verse Jesus speaks of our responsibility to love those who are His followers. As the body of Christ we have a special bond with one another that distinguishes us from those apart from Christ. This doesn't mean we shouldn't love unbelievers. Christ loved us when we were unbelievers, but the majority of the one-another commands are directed toward our brothers in Christ. In considering who we should offer to sell the extra fruits of our farms, our brothers in Christ should be considered of first importance after we have taken care of our families and ourselves.

OUR NEIGHBORS

The entire law is summed up in a single command: "Love your neighbor as yourself. (Galatians 5:14)

We also have a responsibility to love our neighbors. Neighbor refers to those near to us and I believe includes more than just fellow believers. In Luke 10, when a teacher of the law asked Jesus to define "neighbor", He responded with the story of a Samaritan (the Samaritans were a subsection of the Jews that other Jews looked down upon because they had intermarried with non-Jews). This Samaritan helped an injured man who had been robbed, while a Levite and a priest ignored him.

I define a neighbor as someone that the Lord has placed in my life, either through geographic region or circumstance. Does that mean someone on the other side of the world isn't my neighbor? Of course not. But it seems that our responsibility to care for a neighbor is increased by the neighbor's proximity to our lives. I don't believe that this means it's wrong to sell and ship food to people in other places, but I think we need to guard against neglecting the people in our own neighborhoods in order to sell everything we produce to more profitable markets.

During the first several years of the start-up of our farm we have sold primarily in a large city about fifty miles away. However, my goal has been to gradually build more local markets. Last year I started offering vegetables to neighbors on my rural road and ended up selling almost all of my produce in the neighborhood. It doesn't make sense for me to be trucking my produce an hour away when there are people that need it right next door!

3. It's Always our Duty to Share with the Needy

As Christian farmers we have a responsibility to help provide for the needy. This is not third on our priority list; in fact, I don't believe it *has* a priority. It's our duty no matter what. Regardless of how much our farms produce, we should always give a percentage of it to the needy.

Examples of this in Scripture include:

THE TITHE

> At the end of every three years, bring all the *tithes* of that year's produce and store it in your towns, so that *the Levites* (who have no allotment or inheritance of their own) and *the aliens, the fatherless*

and *the widows* who live in your towns *may come and eat and be satis-fied,* and so that the LORD your God may bless you in all the work of your hands. (Deuteronomy 14:28–29)

GLEANING

When you reap the harvest of your land, do not reap to the very edges of your field or gather the gleanings of your harvest. Do not go over your vineyard a second time or pick up the grapes that have fallen. *Leave them for the poor and the alien.* I am the LORD your God. (Leviticus 19:9–10)

ONE GOAL OF WORK IS TO BE ABLE TO SHARE WITH THE NEEDY

He who has been stealing must steal no longer, but must *work,* doing something useful with his own hands, that he may have something to *share* with those in *need.* (Ephesians 4:28)

GENERAL REFERENCES

A generous man will himself be blessed, for he *shares his food with the poor.* (Proverbs 22:9)

There will always be poor people in the land. Therefore I command you to *be openhanded* toward your brothers and *toward the poor and needy* in your land. (Dueteronomy 15:11)

Recently I have begun to try and do a better job of sharing my produce with the needy in our area. Several of our neighbors are widows and I started taking veggies and eggs to some of them.

BIBLICAL CHARACTERISTICS OF MARKETING

Lets look at a few principles that might help define what the marketing of our farm products should look like.

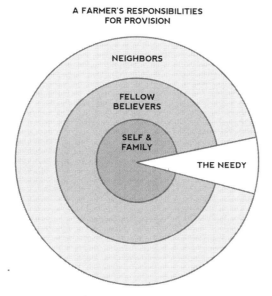

A FARMER'S RESPONSIBILITIES
FOR PROVISION

Relationship-Based

If the marketing we do is to be rooted in love, then it needs to be relationship based. Love involves doing things for one another and looking out for the interest of others. It's hard to do those things without having some sort of relationship. If the people that you sell your farm products to are just numbers on a sheet, it's hard to know how to serve them. In order to adequately know how to serve someone, you really need to know them. For this reason I believe that it's best for most farmers to sell retail as much as possible. There are definitely times for selling wholesale, but you lose a lot of opportunity for ministry. When we sell our corn or chickens to a large, wholesale buyer it's easy to just start thinking about our production in terms of profit, instead of service to others. Actually knowing your customer helps you realize that the food (or fiber) you are producing is actually going to provide for people like you. It's easier to apply the golden rule when we can actually see what we are doing unto others.

Local

In order to effectively have relationships with our customers our marketing should be primarily targeted locally. This means that the majority of food production and distribution would be community based and the focus of the marketing of each farm's produce would be to the people of its local community and region.

Many people think that a local food economy is great to have in the country, but not practical in the city. That's not entirely true. First, we have examples of places like Cuba, where in most cases 80–100% of the fruits and vegetables eaten are grown *in and around the cities!* Even the capitol city of Havana, with a population of 2.5 million, grows 50% of its own produce.

Secondly, at the end of the book of Ezekiel, when God gives dimensions for the division of the land around Jerusalem He sets aside a large portion of land for the production of food for the city:

> The *pastureland for the city* will be 250 cubits on the north, 250 cubits on the south, 250 cubits on the east, and 250 cubits on the west. What remains of the area, bordering on the sacred portion and running the length of it, will be 10,000 cubits on the east side and 10,000 cubits on the west side. Its *produce* will supply *food* for the workers of the *city*. The workers from the *city* who *farm* it will come from all the tribes of Israel. (Ezekiel 48:17–19)

Sabbath-Honoring

In addition to serving the needs of our neighbors, our marketing should honor God's principle of resting on every seventh day. Sometimes a chef will ask me if I want to drop some eggs off on Sunday afternoon. Since that is my day of rest, I just decline. God has given us the gift of rest and I don't want to spoil it by marketing on the Sabbath. It's hard, however, when people ask me about buying things when I am at church. My preference is to just leave something like that until later if possible. If a neighbor really needs something, I am not opposed to giving them something, but that is an act of caring, not working.

In those days I saw men in Judah treading winepresses on the Sabbath and bringing in *grain* and loading it on donkeys, together with *wine, grapes, figs* and all other kinds of loads. And they were bringing all this into Jerusalem *on the Sabbath.* Therefore I warned them against selling food *on that day.* (Nehemiah 13:15)

In addition to serving the needs of our neighbors, our marketing should honor God's principle of resting on every seventh day.

WHAT ARE SOME PRACTICAL WAYS TO PROVIDE FRUITS TO MY NEIGHBOR?

A FARMERS' MARKET

One good way to offer the products of your farm to your neighbors is through a local farmers market. The market is a place where farmers set up on particular days and display their produce to interested shoppers. These markets are becoming more common than they once were and attendance seems to be rising. Our farm sells much of its produce at a local farmers market.

PROS	CONS
• Provides great way to build relationships with people	• No guarantee that you will sell anything
• Flexible—if you don't have anything to bring, no obligation	• Weather can affect sales
• Provides customers	• Takes a lot of time for packing, setting up, selling, and breaking down

- Very little driving around compared to making deliveries

- Other competition may have already filled certain needs

A Farm Stand

A farm stand is like having your own personal farmers market on your farm. You can just set up a table, display your produce on it, and make some signs telling what you have. Neighbors can just come right to your farm and buy produce.

PROS	CONS
• No driving	• Normally fewer customers than a market with more selection
• Very little set up and breaking down if stand is more permanent.	• Liability with customers coming on the farm
• You can go pick more veggies if you run out at the stand	
• Less competition	
• An "honor-box" can be used, depending on where you live.	
• You set your own hours	
• Customers can see the farm where their food is grown	

Community Supported Agriculture (CSA)

One of the best ways to build relationships with your customers is through Community-Supported Agriculture. CSA is a subscription type marketing model where you sell seasonal memberships to your farm. Members receive weekly "shares" of whatever the farm is producing at the time, either delivered or picked up. There are many variations of this model. One variation I hope to see developed someday is Church-Supported Agriculture, where members of the Body of Christ join together to support born-again farmers!

PROS	CONS
• Provides guaranteed and predictable sales	• Obligation to fill shares brings added pressure to produce
• Allows you to plan ahead more accurately	• Complexity of managing members and pickups/ deliveries
• Gives opportunity for strong farmer-consumer relationship	
• Less time spent marketing	
• Members get more vegetables for their money	

Peddling

Especially if you have extra produce to sell, peddling door-to-door is a great way to make it available to people. Of course, it helps to have a fairly outgoing personality. My father-in-law sold a lot of vegetables one season by driving around to different businesses and doctors offices. Another man I am friends with makes his living peddling fruits and vegetables that he buys from farmers. The key is trying to provide people with what they need, not just hawking your wares. Nobody likes to be pressured into buying something. Though peddling may not the best full time marketing model for most farmers, it can be a good backup one.

PROS	CONS
• Some people who wouldn't go out of their way to buy your products will purchase them if you have them right there	• It takes a lot of driving
	• Some places don't allow solicitors
• You can be proactive about making your produce available to people, rather than sitting and hoping they come to you	• Uncertainty of sales

LOCAL RESTAURANTS

Another local market that has really opened up in recent years is that of local restaurants. Many chefs are beginning to look for fresh produce grown locally because their customers desire it. This is an opportunity to be able to help them out by giving them access to high quality products that they can provide to their diners.

PROS	CONS
• Chefs tend to buy more at one time than an individual	• Pays a little less because it's more wholesale

- Very little marketing time, just call for orders and deliver

- Can take overflow from other markets at times

- Some chefs can be more picky than others

- Less relationship with the people who actually eat your food

- Some localities have codes and regulations prohibiting direct sales. Special licenses may be required

LOCAL STORES

One type of local wholesale markets that still provides a sort of relationship with your "neighbors" is small, privately owned grocery stores. When our farmer's market season is over we continue to provide products like eggs to our customers at several "organic" grocery stores nearby. We sell these eggs directly to the store, not to a wholesale buyer, which allows us to build a relationship with the store managers. It also gives the people who shop there access to straight-from-the-farm produce.

PROS	CONS
• Stores will buy large quantities of products and do the individual selling for you	• Pays a little less because it's more wholesale
	• Much lower, wholesale price

- Less marketing time. Just call for orders and drop off

- Year round market

- Sometimes more processing of produce. We have to grade and weigh eggs we sell to stores

- Less interaction with the consumers

PRICING AND PROFITABILITY

One of the difficulties of retail selling to your neighbors is that you have to decide what to charge them. In a sense this is great because it means that you are a price maker instead of a price taker (you're a price taker when you sell somewhere like a grain elevator). But today I see two extremes of pricing that most of us farmers tend to gravitate toward.

One extreme that is easy for Christian farmers to fall into is charging too little. This is especially easy if you sell retail. If we desire to serve others and build relationships with our customers, we can begin to feel guilty charging them full price. We tend to feel more holy if we charge less than something is worth. However, this mindset can easily cause our farms to be unprofitable and wasteful.

The other extreme is always trying to charge as much as you can get away with. Obviously this is greedy and doesn't consider the other person's interests.

How do we know what God wants us to charge? Here are a few principles that might give us a biblical perspective on pricing and profitability:

FOR GOOD STEWARDSHIP, OUR PRICES MUST MAKE A PROFIT

If our prices don't allow us to produce more than we consume, then we are being poor stewards. A good steward doesn't waste or just retain his master's property—he adds to it. In the parable of the talents in Matthew 25, the master entrusts his servants with certain sums of money. Upon his return, the servants who had used their money to earn more receive a "well done!" But the servant who had merely kept his money was punished for being wasteful. Therefore the products of our farm should make a profit, adding to the value of the resources God has given to us. Profitable pricing benefits our customers, because it allows us to stay in business and continue to serve them with our products.

PROFIT IS A REFLECTION OF THE INCREASE GOD ADDS TO OUR WORK

Where does profit come from? If we start with a limited amount of time and resources, and profit adds to them, then that extra has to come from somewhere! There are two options:

- Profit comes at the expense of others.

- Profit is the result of the increase supplied by God.

The first option is one of the reasons that we feel guilty about charging someone more than it cost us. We feel that we are somehow unfairly profiting from them. This may be the case in some businesses, but shouldn't be in agriculture. When we plant a crop we invest seeds, equipment time, labor, and perhaps other resources like soil amendments and water. From one little seed grows a plant that can produce hundreds more seeds. That miracle of that increase is the result of the blessing and abundance of God.

> Isaac planted crops in that land and the same year reaped a hundredfold, *because the LORD blessed him.* (Genesis 26:12)

If we just view the value of the crops and animals that we produce as equivalent to what we put into them, then we are denying the increase that God has given. Therefore our prices should reflect that value of the increase God has given. It is really confounding that farmers can plant seeds in the ground, harvest a hundred times more than we planted, and still lose money!

THE INCREASE GOD GIVES SHOULD BE SHARED WITH OTHERS

The beauty of the increase that God gives to the work of our hands is that it provides enough for the farmer to sell at a profit and still share the abundance with the consumer. Hypothetically speaking, let's say that you planted $1 worth of seed and spent $29 in production and labor caring for it, and God blessed you with a hundredfold harvest. For the $30 you invested, the Lord technically gave you an increase of $70 worth of crop. However, you don't want to be greedy with God's increase. You want to use it to bless others. Therefore you can sell your crop for something less than its $100 value, say $65, and both you and your customer share in the abundance ($35 apiece). God's abundance allows a sale to be a win-win situation because both you and your customer receive some of the increase. How much of the increase you share with the customer can vary. When selling wholesale, you normally pass on a larger percentage of the increase so the middlemen can have enough to make a profit. When you sell retail you get to keep more of the increase.

Here are some particular applications of these principles:

- Don't be afraid to charge a fair price for your farm products. Many people will complain about prices because our society has been spoiled with deceptively low prices due to subsidies and poor quality food. Explain to customers what it takes to grow good food and that you aren't gouging them.

- If you can't make a profit on something at a fair price, then stop growing it or find a way to cut costs.

- If you are charging what you are confident is a fair price, then don't lower it if someone tries to dicker with you. *Either charge full price, or give it away.* If a customer at the market asks you for a deal, tell them honestly that you believe the price you are asking is fair, and to lower it would be misrepresenting its value. If it appears that they need something and can't afford it, then give it to them if the Lord leads you to do so. I have tried to make it a policy at our market to give a half dozen eggs to anyone that walks away muttering about the price. After experiencing the quality of the eggs the customers almost always come back for more.

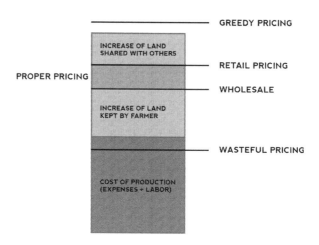

PROPER PRICING OF FARM PRODUCTS

WHAT ARE SOME BENEFITS OF PROVIDING FRUITS TO OUR NEIGHBORS?

RELIABILITY

A more local food economy is not as affected by outside events as an economy is that imports its food from far away. A war on the other side of the world, a drought in another state, or high fuel prices have much less impact on food grown and consumed within a community or region. The food supply of the consumer is much more secure, as are the markets for the farmer. Also, the necessity of growing a diversity of crops to meet the needs of local people means there is less likelihood of all the crops failing.

ACCOUNTABILITY

When you know who is eating the food that you grow, you are much less likely to take shortcuts that impact quality, not only because you care about your neighbors, but also because they will stop buying from you if you have bad products. When customers know where their food is coming from, they are held accountable in their purchasing decisions by a better understanding of who they are supporting. When produce is shared with those who are needy, the recipients of the charity can be held accountable to work and improve their lives if it is within their power.

SUSTAINABILITY

Offering the products of our farms to our neighbors also provides the benefit of sustainability—sustainability in the sense that the system is using resources at a rate that can be sustained. First of all, selling locally utilizes local resources and is not too dependent upon outside inputs. Less distance from the farm to the consumer means less transportation costs. When the farmers are eating what they produce, little is wasted. (We eat all the cracked eggs from our hens). Farms that create many different products because of local demand often utilize farm resources more effectively.

CONCLUSION

Marketing is an important part of the success of our farms. We should give much thought and prayer to our marketing method. Marketing involves interacting with those in our community and can provide a good testimony for Christ or a bad one. It's a great opportunity to share the love of Christ with our families, the Church, and our communities. Marketing is ministry. As we provide products to people in our communities, God provides opportunities to build up relationships and share the love of Christ.

10

AGRI-LIFESTYLE

Is farming really worth it?

"THERE AIN'T NO MONEY IN FARMING ANYMORE."

"You can't make a living farming."

"Do you want to know how to make a small fortune farming? Start off with a large one!"

Commonly-heard statements like these can be discouraging at times for those of us who desire to be stewards of God's land and grow good food for people. American society generally looks down upon the calling of farmer. No one encourages young people to become farmers. A young farmer selling across from me at the market said his dad (who farms) wouldn't let his son "just farm." He had to go to college and get a real job because, "There ain't no money in farming anymore!" Plus, farming is hard work, risky, and it ties you down when there are plenty of other jobs where you can make money a lot easier.

Why is it so hard to make a living farming? It's one of the most productive occupations, seemingly producing something from nothing, yet it is one of the most poorly-paid occupations. Today you can invest half a million dollars in a chicken house in hopes of making twenty thousand dollars a year. That's a pretty poor return on your investment compared to most businesses.

The Impact of Government on Farming Profitability

One of the biggest factors in farming unprofitability today is government intervention. In his eye-opening book, *War on the Poor*, historian Clarence B. Carson claimed that "there is no reason, except for government interference, that farming should not be as profitable an undertaking as any other productive pursuit".[1] Why is the government's intervention such a bad thing?

First, the annual welfare that the government doles out each year to "help" farmers that are struggling promotes mediocre farming. As I said earlier in this book, when the government helps keep unprofitable farmers in business, it tends to put all the profitable farmers out of business. If my neighbor is being a bad farmer and wastes his resources such that he loses money, instead of eventually going out of business and making room for someone who will be a better steward of his farm, he stays in business. He can sell at a loss, undercut me, and go on year after year because of government subsidies. Most commodity farmers don't undercut on purpose. They have to take whatever the market price is at the time. The market price reflects the fact that farmers can sell crops at less than the price of production and still make a profit because of subsidies. If there were no subsidies and farmers stopped growing crops they couldn't sell profitably, then the prices would soon rise to a realistic level that would allow for profitable production.

"[T]here is no reason...that farming should not be as profitable an undertaking as any other productive pursuit."

Second, government regulation of food production and processing makes it difficult to sell any type of meat produced by a small-scale, entry level farmer. These regulations are designed for a system in which farmers take whatever wholesale price they can get while selling to a large company. The best way to make money on a small farm is direct sales, which regulations inhibit. There are creative ways to deal with this, as farmer Joel Salatin has helped show in his book *Everything I Want to Do is Illegal*. When compliance with government regulations is practical only for large corporations (who can absorb

---

1   Carson, Clarence B. *War on the Poor.* New Rochelle: Arlington House (1969), 116.

the cost) it limits the options of most small producers. Government inter-ference has resulted in the drastic decline of the family farm, a debt-based agricultural production model, and a lack of new farmers. It has made the occupation of farming unattractive compared to other pursuits and has made it very hard to start farming. Still, it's possible to make a living farming because many people are doing it, including me. With God all things really are possible if they are according to His will.

HOPE FOR CHRISTIAN FARMERS

How do we respond as Christian farmers? Do we just sigh and say like everyone else, "Well, I guess there ain't no money in farming anymore," and resign ourselves to farming as a hobby? Do we quit altogether?

No. Despite the intervention of the government and the lack of fi-nancial return on agriculture, I believe farming is still a worthwhile pursuit.

First, I believe that someday farming will again be recognized and rewarded as one of the most fundamental and essential endeavors in our economy. It's not unlikely that the current industrial system of ag-riculture will someday fail because of its dependence on so many other inputs, one of which is oil. If it does fail people will still need food. Growing food will quickly rise to the top of the list of valued skills.

This is exactly what happened in Cuba in the 1990s. When the USSR collapsed and the U.S. imposed its embargoes, Cuba's economy collapsed because there were almost no imports, including oil. Cuba's agriculture, which was very industrialized, began to falter for lack of fertilizer, chemicals, and fuel and parts for tractors. Food became scarce. The average Cuban lost twenty pounds those first several years. Soon people began to try to grow food. Abandoned lots in the city were cleaned up and planted for food. Large, state-owned farms were divided up between small farmers. People who had been professional business people switched to agriculture. Today, Cuba grows the majori-ty of its own food. Farming is one of the most profitable professions be-cause farmers have food that people want to buy and the farmers don't have to buy food themselves. One Cuban farmer, who was formerly a musician, mechanic, and electronics designer, now makes his living growing food on the roof of his house in the city.[2]

With the current violation of God's principles of economics by our government, I believe that America could easily face the same challenges that Cuba faced. Farming would once again be a valuable skill for Christians to have.

Second, if we as Christian farmers begin to glorify the Lord in the way we farm, using His wisdom and applying His principles, I believe our farms can be so productive that we can make a profit despite the intervention of government. God is the best farmer in the whole world—in the whole universe in fact!—and if we learn from Him I believe we can eventually beat the socks off the worldly producers of today.

Third, the reward of farming is more than just money. One of the biggest benefits of farming is the lifestyle it offers. When I get up to work in the morning I am not motivated by the amount of money I will make that day. I actually rarely think about it. Instead, I am enjoying the work God has given me of caring for and working His creation while walking with Him, enjoying relationships with my family, displaying the Gospel to those around me, and providing for my needs. Farming to me is a lifestyle of ministry and worship. I guess you could describe what I do more accurately as agri-lifestyle, rather than agri-business.

LIFESTYLE ENTREPRENEURSHIP

I want to address the difference between what I would call "moneymaking entrepreneurship" and "lifestyle entrepreneurship."

Moneymaking entrepreneurship is what most people think of when they think of entrepreneurship. Basically you come up with a business idea based on whether you think it will be successful at making money, and you start it. Hopefully you will make money and after the business has grown to a certain point you will be able to hire others to run it or sell it and you'll be able to afford to live the lifestyle that you want. The best moneymaking business is one that provides the most amount of money with the least amount of effort.

---

2 For further information, see www.powerofcommunity.org.

The lifestyle entrepreneur sacrifices the probability of making big money for the pleasure of meaningful work. The work is the primary reward. Ultimately, the goal of both types of entrepreneurship is the ability to be able to have the type of lifestyle desired. Moneymaking entrepreneurs seek to find a business doing something that they don't necessarily like in order to be able to live a desired lifestyle at a later time. Lifestyle entrepreneurs seek to find ways to make a living doing what they want to do in the first place.

Because of the time, devotion, care, and work that it takes to farm (in addition to the government's negative impact) it doesn't qualify very well as a pure moneymaking business. There's too much work for the pay if you would rather be doing something else. In the future, this may change if there is a shortage of food, but because of the beautiful work setting, the opportunity to work with your hands, the ability to spend time with family, and the satisfaction one gets from growing things, farming makes a great lifestyle that can provide for the needs of the worker and the needs of others.

One of the biggest benefits of farming is the lifestyle it offers.

AGRI-BUSINESS VS. AGRI-LIFESTYLE

So let's take a look at the difference between agri-business and agri-lifestyle.

Agri-business views farming from the viewpoint of "moneymaking entrepreneurship." It's asking the question, "How can my farm make enough money to support the lifestyle I desire?" Success is viewed in terms of how much money is made. Profit and yield drives most of the decisions made. Seldom is a decision made based on improving the lifestyle of the farmer. Many of the agri-business models tend to be corporate, centralized, debt-based, and very large scale.

Agri-lifestyle on the other hand, views farming from the viewpoint of "lifestyle entrepreneurship." It values the lifestyle opportunities that agriculture presents and seeks to take advantage of those, in a sense viewing them as part of the "income" received from the farm. Success is viewed in terms of whether or not the farm is creating a desirable lifestyle. Agri-lifestyle tends to be family-based, decentralized, small-scale, and debt-free.

As we saw in Chapter Two, one of the foundations for a biblical agricultural worldview is the fact that farming's not about us, but rather about bringing Glory to God and serving others. Though money can be helpful in accomplishing those things, I believe that God intends for us to do them directly, in everything we do.

This is helpful for me to think about, especially when business people I respect are skeptical about the viability of a farm as a business. When they hold my agri-lifestyle farm up to the standard of a money-making business, it fails miserably, compared to other things I could be doing. Why would I be doing something that requires manual labor and brings in less than minimum wage for my time? Shouldn't I be starting an online business or something? Because farming supplies much of what I need to live a Godly life, I don't need much money. Yes, I want to be productive, but God doesn't judge productivity just based on money. He judges based on the fruit you produce for the Kingdom of God.

THE IMPORTANCE OF AGRI-LIFESTYLE FOR THE FAMILY

It's interesting to note that an agri-lifestyle is very consistent with and supportive of the Biblical model of the family. The abandonment of the agricultural family economy during the industrial revolution is partly responsible for much of the breakdown of the Christian family and morals.

Humanist historians Will and Ariel Durant, well known for their work *The Story of Civilization*, wrote a book to sum up what they had learned from their study called *The Lessons of History*. It's a shocking book revealing the fruits of a Christless worldview. Nevertheless, they made a very good, though twisted, observation of the impact our shift from an agricultural nation to an industrialized nation had on the morals of the family.

In their chapter, "Morals and History", they falsely contend that morals are the natural result of economic and social models. They say that first there was the hunter-gatherer moral code of survival of the fittest, then the agricultural moral code, then the industrial moral code. What is interesting to me is that they attribute the Christian standard of ethics to the agricultural code because of the way an agrarian lifestyle fits with the biblical model of family. Here is a quote:

> Children were economic assets; birth control was made immoral. On the farm the family was the unit of production under the discipline of the father and the seasons, and paternal authority had a firm economic base. Each normal son matured soon in mind and self-support; at fifteen he understood the physical tasks of life as well as he would understand them at forty; all that he needed was land, a plow, and a willing arm. So he married early, almost as soon as nature wished; he did not fret long under the restraints placed upon premarital relations by the new order of permanent settlements and homes. As for young women, chastity was indispensable, for its loss might bring unprotected motherhood. Monogamy was demanded by the approximate numerical equality of the sexes. For fifteen hundred years this agricultural moral code of continence, early marriage, divorceless monogamy, and multiple maternity maintained itself in Christian Europe and its white colonies. It was a stern code, which produced some of the strongest characters in history.[3]

I believe that the Durants had it backwards. Instead of the view that a family-based, agrarian lifestyle results in Christian morals, it could be viewed that Christian morals result in the former. It's also interesting to note their description of the destruction of the family and Christian morals through the rise of industrialism.

> Gradually, then rapidly and ever more widely, the Industrial Revolution changed the economic form and moral superstructure of European and American life. Men, women, and children left the home and family, authority and unity, to work as individuals, individually paid, in factories built to house not men, but machines. Every decade the machines multiplied and became more complex; economic maturity (the capacity to support a family) came later;

---

3   Will Durant and Ariel Durant, *The Lessons of History*. New York: Simon & Schuster (2010), 38–39.

children no longer were economic assets; marriage was delayed; premarital continence became more difficult to maintain. The city offered every discouragement to marriage, but it provided every stimulus and facility for sex. Women were "emancipated"—i.e., industrialized....The authority of father and mother lost its economic base through the growing individualism of industry. The rebellious youth was no longer constrained by the surveillance of the village; he could hide his sins in the protective anonymity of the city crowd. The progress of science raised the authority of the test tube over that of the crosier; the mechanization of economic production suggested mechanistic materialistic philosophies: education spread religious doubts; morality lost more and more of its supernatural supports. The old agricultural moral code began to die.[4]

What can we learn from this? I don't believe that farming is the only profession, or a "sacred" profession for Christians, but I *do* believe that it's one of the most foundational. Farming is a fundamental application of a family economy; an economy based upon productive families working together. This is what we see in the garden of Eden: a family placed in a garden, working together and producing fruit for the glory of God.

We need to realize the impact the man-centered industrial revolution has had on the family. We should consider a return to God-centered, family-based economic models. We should look for models in which families can work together for the kingdom of God, building relationships, encouraging one another, and providing accountability and a glorious testimony to the world around them. Almost any type of work can be viable in building God-glorifying family economies, but I believe that the reformation of our economy to rebuild Christian families needs to start with recapturing the work of the soil, even if it means the sacrifice of some income for some of us.

---

4   *ibid.*, 39.

How Does Farming Promote a Biblical Lifestyle?

Let's look at how Christian farming and an agri-lifestyle can help produce the kind of fruit God desires.

Some of the things important to a Biblical lifestyle would be: fearing God (Psalm 34:9), ruling His creation (Genesis 1:28), ministering to our families (1 Timothy 3:4; Ephesians 5:33, 6:1–4), ministering to believers (John 13:35), and ministering to unbelievers outside our family (Matthew 5:43–45).

How can an agricultural lifestyle help us to focus on the aforementioned biblical mandates?

FEARING GOD

As Christian farmers, it's our responsibility to fear the Lord, to walk with Him, to realize our dependence upon Him, growing in love and obedience toward Him. There are several ways Christian farming can facilitate this.

- First, farming promotes a trust in God because we are directly dependent on Him to produce fruit. God is our ultimate provider no matter what occupation we have, but sometimes it's easy to forget when we are looking to an employer or boss. In farming God's provision is more visible because it comes straight from the ground.

- Farming enables us to learn more of God as we work with His creation. Romans 1:20 says, "For since the creation of the world God's invisible qualities—his eternal power and divine nature—have been clearly seen, being understood from what has been made, so that men are without excuse." When I see the beauty of a squash blossom or the wisdom in the design of the veins of a leaf, or see the power of roots in breaking up the soil, I am learning more about my Creator. Everything good we see is a small glimpse of our Heavenly Father. Walking around our farm can be a form of agri-seminary if we allow our eyes to be opened by the Holy Spirit.

- I have found that farming provides many opportunities to enjoy walking with the Lord in a more open way than most environments allow. When I am working in the garden or doing the chores, I can pray out loud and sing praises to the Lord. Lately I have been singing to the rhythm of the milk streaming into the bucket as I milk our cow. When I am presented with a dilemma or problem I can ask, even audibly, for God to give me wisdom.

- People say that farmers are self-employed. This isn't true. We are employed directly by God. We have freedom to apply the principles of Scripture to the way we live and work. When we work for someone else we have to do what they say, while acting in a moral, Christian way. When we work for God we have the opportunity to apply a biblical worldview to every aspect of our work. As farmers we have the luxury of being able to ask, "What would be a more God-honoring way to graze this pasture?" Or, "How can I reflect the care of God in the way I build this chicken coop?"

RULING CREATION

In the very beginning God gave man the responsibility of ruling His creation by caring for it and working it. Farming helps us to be about these tasks in several obvious ways:

- First, farming helps us to rule creation in a very direct and basic way. I am attempting to "rule" creation as I write this book. By typing on a laptop I am utilizing part of the creation to produce fruit. Farming is, however, a more fundamental way to rule the earth.

- Second, farming enables us to better rule creation because we are able to see first-hand the results of our care and work. We are able to benefit from, or reap the consequences of, our stewardship in a very direct way. When we plant seeds, we see (Lord willing) the fruits of our labors. When we fail to care for our animals we see the ill effects. This first-hand knowledge of the result of our stewardship provides accountability and motivation in our work of ruling creation.

- I also believe that farming enables us to do a good job of ruling creation because we get to work with our hands. In ruling creation we are reflecting the image of God in the work we do. The Scriptures often refer to creation as the work of God's hand (Isaiah 45:12). Therefore, it would make sense that one of the best ways we could reflect the image of God in the way we rule creation is by working with our hands.

MINISTERING TO FAMILY

As we respond to the call to love and serve others, our family comes first. Out of all the people in the world they come marked as our assignment. The family should be a body of loving relationships, a productive team that works together in their respective roles to advance the Kingdom of God. What are some ways farming promotes the ministry of the family?

- Born-again farming helps promote the family by allowing the father and husband to work at home. As the head of the family, we fathers are responsible for leading, discipling, protecting, and providing for our families. In my opinion this is best done when we don't have to spend most of the day away from our families. Working on my farm allows me to disciple my family when we rise up and when we lie down and as we walk in the way (Deuteronomy 6).

  Working on my farm allows me to disciple my family when we rise up and when we lie down and when we walk in the way.

- Farming promotes family because it enables the family to be able to work together. In my experience, when you work and accomplish something with somebody, your hearts are drawn together and your relationship strengthened. When husbands and wives can work together, God can strengthen their marriage. When

children work with their parents, they can learn and be
discipled in preparation for having families of their own
one day. When siblings can work with each other they
learn to value one another and practice living in love
with others (because siblings aren't perfect!). Recently
my wife and I took turns helping with the other person's
work. I helped her in the kitchen and mixed up bread
dough and she helped me load up an egg order. It was
great being able to be together while we were working,
and we got a lot done working as a team.

- Farming promotes the family unit because it allows everyone to contribute to the family instead of just consuming. Because of the diversity of work and abundance
of simple manual labor, everyone can contribute. From
the diapered toddler picking beans, to the wheelchair-
bound grandparent snapping them. When everyone can
work on the same projects there is less disconnect between the generations and more opportunities for prac-
ticing love and service. There are other types of work
besides farming that men can do from home, but many
of these are not types of work that the whole family can
participate in.

MINISTERING TO OTHERS

As individuals and families God desires our lives to be about sharing
His love with others. First to our brothers in Christ, and then to our
unbelieving neighbors. The great thing about farming is that it gives
us many opportunities to serve and share the gospel with others.

- Farming helps us minister to others by producing food
and fiber to meet basic physical needs. We can go all out
in producing high quality food because it needs to be
something we would want to eat ourselves. When I go to
sell my produce I often feel that it's a ministry more than
a job.

- Second, a Christian farm (a beautiful, fruitful home) provides a great opportunity to minister to others through
hospitality. This is one thing that God has allowed us to

do with our farm. It's really a rare week when we don't have at least one person come and visit or stay with us. We have people come from our church, our community, and our farmers' market. Normally they eat at least one meal with us and get a farm tour, as well as helping us work. During these times we are able to talk about and do things that we wouldn't be able to do as easily outside of our home. I get to encourage many young men who love to come and do "farm work."

- Because farming is more of a lifestyle than just a business, it's a great opportunity to let our lives shine as testimonies of the gospel. Whether we are working in the field, selling at the market, buying feed, or whatever, we can display the sanctifying work of God's grace in our lives. People notice. Time and time again people comment on the good behavior and communication skills of my younger brothers at the farmers' market, an excellent opportunity to give credit to the Lord for the fruits evident in our lives.

WHAT ARE SOME BENEFITS OF A FARMING LIFESTYLE?

Too often you hear people talk about all the downsides of farming—the risk, the work, the hardships. We Christian farmers need to stop being blinded by our lack of faith and selfishness and recognize all the wonderful blessings of the work and lifestyle God has given us. Here are a few I have noticed:

INTEGRATION OF ALL AREAS OF LIFE
INSTEAD OF FRAGMENTATION

When God placed man in the garden his life consisted of his relationship with God, the work God gave him to do, and his relationship with his family. These three areas of life were integrated.

When farming is more of a lifestyle than a business separate from the rest of your life, it simplifies the hectic schedules most people endure by integrating the different areas of their lives. I'm talking specifically about the different areas mentioned above: Our relationship with God, our taking dominion of creation, and our ministering to our family and to others.

Integration is possible in many types of work if the work is family-based, but farming is especially suited to applying an integrated lifestyle of worship because of the nature of the work and the freedom it offers. For instance, if I am weeding the garden with my wife or son, while singing songs to the Lord, I am walking with the Lord, ruling His creation, and ministering to my family all at the same time!

OPPORTUNITY FOR DISCIPLESHIP OF
CHILDREN (OR YOUNG PEOPLE)

I want to mention again that one of the blessings of farming is the ability to effectively disciple our children. This is one of the main reasons that I farm. Right now my son is only a few months old, but already I have experienced the advantages of being home for almost every meal and being able to begin training him. I look forward to being able to take him with me while I work and begin teaching him the ways of the Lord. I plan on homeschooling my children. Education isn't something you do just sitting at a desk; it's a *lifestyle*. I want to be able to help my son become a man of God, by being an example to him. I want him to learn responsibility, to see first-hand that diligence and hard work bring a profit, but laziness leads to poverty. The discipleship opportunities a farming lifestyle offers are legion, if we will take advantage of them.

Multi-Generational Impact

Another blessing of an agri-lifestyle is the impact that it can have on multiple generations. The increased opportunity for discipleship can have a significant impact on the next generation. Multi-generational family property also enables one generation to set up monuments for spiritual remembrance. Each generation can invest in the next by leaving the farm more reformed to Scripture and more fruitful. Young men can begin to learn skills and contribute to the farm at an early age, enabling them to prepare for families of their own. The ability to share resources on a farm can give the next generation a head start. The older generation can also continue to be productive by having work that they can do at a comfortable pace, maximizing their limited energy and strength.

Healthful Living

As a farmer you are producing and eating fresh, high quality food and getting good, daily exercise. Of course, if you aren't basing your farm on God's principles and you use lots of chemicals, it might not be healthy for you. Factory farming can be very dangerous because of the emphasis on high production, trying to squeeze every last penny out of the land. A Christian perspective of depending on God for provision can help the farmer work at a safe, reasonable pace. Done right, farming is one of the best professions for your body. I once saw a list of life expectancies for different occupations in an old business handbook from the late 19th century. Clerks had the lowest life expectancy, somewhere in the early thirties, and farmers were at the top of the list—with a life expectancy in the seventies, even back in the 19th century.

Education isn't just something you do sitting at a desk; it's a LIFESTYLE.

CONCLUSION

The production of food and fiber from the soil isn't a profession that can be outdated. Despite low profit due to government meddling we can't just say that it isn't worth doing any more. If farming dies, so do we! Instead, we need to realize that farming has more to offer than just money. We must encourage Christian farmers in the pursuit of a God-glorifying agri-lifestyle.

My goal isn't to make anyone feel hindered or inferior if they do something other than farming. In order to be a good farmer you really have to love farming, and not everyone does. There are many other pursuits that can provide opportunities for a godly lifestyle. My desire is that Christians of all professions will begin to look at their work as more than just a means of making money. Our job is to seek first His Kingdom and all these things (the necessities of life) will be added to us.

11

GETTING STARTED: TIPS AND SUGGESTIONS

How can we start or support Born-Again Dirt?

I WANT TO CONCLUDE THIS BOOK BY PROVIDING YOU WITH SOME PRAC-tical tips for starting a farm, making a living on a farm, and making the transition from worldly farming to Christian farming. I also want to provide advice for young men getting started in farming, and en-couragement for non-farmers who want to see the dirt born again.

PRACTICAL TIPS FOR STARTING A FARM

The Lord is raising up a new generation of Christian farmers. Families like mine are moving back to the land to experience some of the bless-ings of an agrarian lifestyle. Because this is new to most of us, it can be difficult to know where to begin. Based on our experience so far, here are a few things we recommend you consider when starting a farm.

ESTABLISH A VISION

Vision has to do with where you are going and how you plan to get there. Where do you want your farm to go? More importantly, where does God want it to go? What will your farm look like in one year? Five years? Ten?

I have found that it's helpful to think of vision as a direction rather than just a set of goals. If we are too goal-oriented, it's easy to lose sight of the fact that, because of sin, we don't ever "arrive" perfectly in anything we do. Direction, however, helps remind us that we are on a journey of sanctification.

In order to establish a vision for your farm, you need to pray, consult Scripture, and consider why and how God would want you to farm. Parts of this book will help you in thinking about it. Describe what your farm will look like. Picture it in twenty years and write a detailed description. See how that description aligns with the reasons God wants you to farm. Then set short-term and long-term goals that will help you accomplish your vision. Remember, try to be direction-driven rather than goal-driven.

START WITH WHAT YOU HAVE

When implementing your vision you must start with what you have. Take the talents the Lord has given you and put them to work. Be faithful with little before you expect the Lord to bless you with much.

When I first started farming my family lived on eleven acres, and most of it was wooded. During the first few years I took parts of that land and began raising chickens for eggs and meat, planting gardens, and keeping bees, all on a small-scale. This was wise, because my mistakes didn't cost as much. Start small, lose small. Prove yourself faithful with little before expanding into bigger things.

EXPAND AS THE LORD ENABLES (PREFERABLY WITHOUT DEBT)

When you are growing a farm, it's very important to avoid debt if at all possible. Basically you want to expand your farm at a rate that matches the skills, resources, and markets God has given you. If you expand your production faster than your market or skill levels can handle, you can quickly end up in a hole. I believe that the majority of the time,

God will provide the resources to expand and grow according to His timing.

If you feel that you need to buy a particular piece of equipment or build a certain building, but can't do it without debt, I would seriously pray and ask God if He wants you to make such an investment at this time. The Bible says that debt is slavery (Proverbs 22:7) and warns against voluntarily becoming a slave (1 Corinthians 7:23). Although it is sometimes necessary, I don't believe God desires for our businesses to be based upon debt. If you must have it, debt should be very short-term.

One way to avoid debt is to use scalable production models. For instance, modular animal housing such as small chicken shelters allow you to start with one, and expand indefinitely as your markets grow. This enables you to finance the growth of your operation with capitol earned along the way. I used this principle to expand our chicken operation with great success.

LEARN TO EVALUATE NEW IDEAS

Becoming Godly farmers and farming to His glory is a process of sanctification and we won't ever be done improving in this lifetime. As a Christian farmer I am always looking for new ideas and then holding them up to a Biblical agrarian worldview to see what truth and wisdom I can glean from them. This is what we must learn to do if we are going to have a successful farm.

As Christians our worldview should continually affect the way we work the land. As we start our farms we need to glean as much wisdom as we can from others' experience and from creation, and then filter it through the screen of a Biblical worldview. There are many people out there, even those who deny God, who have done a great job observing the wisdom in creation and utilizing it. We can learn a lot from them, but mustn't accept anything without evaluating it biblically.

HOW CAN YOU MAKE A LIVING ON A FARM?

Many people I know who are interested in farming don't do it as a career. It's more of a part-time pursuit than a primary source of income. Some of them desire to do it full time. They just don't see how they can practically do it. As they consider the income of their current career, it's hard for them to picture their farm replacing it. Many farmers will tell you, "Farming is great, but you can't make a living doing it." Here are some thoughts in response:

First of all, it's hard to make a living farming today. Nothing worth doing comes without work, but government intervention in agriculture has made farming as a vocation especially difficult.

Second, it's good to desire to farm full-time, but don't view yourself as an unsuccessful farmer just because you do other work. It often takes one generation financing the next generation in order to get started. Sometimes other work is needed to help build to the point that the farm can support itself. Don't feel that you have failed as a farmer if you still require other income. The lifestyle is worthwhile and the money you save producing your own food and fiber can help tremendously with expenses.

Third, try to rid yourself of the specialist mindset that our culture has today. Even if you do make your living farming, don't limit your pursuits to just agriculture. Historically, many farmers were well rounded men that engaged in politics, crafts, trade, and war. Abraham, King David, King Uzziah, Oliver Cromwell, and George Washington were all farmers whose skill in agriculture carried over into the rest of their lives.

Don't view yourself as an unsuccessful farmer just because you do other work.

The question is, "Can you make a living as a Christian farmer?"

The answer is, "It depends on how you live" (just as it does in any other profession).

If you live a consumer lifestyle it can be very difficult to make a living farming, especially when you are first starting out. By consumer lifestyle I mean:

- Lots of debt that limits your flexibility

- The need to buy everything you consume at retail prices

If you live a productive lifestyle, which means producing much of what you need, then it's easier to make a living as a farmer.

During the first few years of farming I have been providing for my family from an $1,100 monthly salary I draw as farm manager. To many people this may not sound like much, but consider that we are starting out living in a small apartment in our farm's shop and have no house payment. We have a small, used car which we own. We grow most of our own food or buy in bulk. We also heat our house in the winter with our wood cook stove as well as cooking on it. Without most of the major expenses most people have, we can comfortably live on $1,100 a month. I plan to increase my salary as the farm becomes more developed and more profitable, but I am able to make a living on what the farm produces right now because I choose to live simply. I am also not opposed to supplementing my income with other complementary pursuits as appropriate or as needed.

One of the keys to being able to provide for your family through your farm is making sure that you make a profit. We must be producing more than we are consuming. In the book of Proverbs we see that the things that lead to profit are planning, hard work, and generosity (Proverbs 14:23, 21:5, 11:24). On the other hand, haste, laziness and stinginess lead to poverty.

As Christian farmers we also realize that it's not ultimately our own ability to plan or our hard work that will enable our farm to provide for our families. It is God Who provides. Because God owns everything and we are stewards, we must accept the fact that even if we are faithful in production and/or marketing, He may have other plans. We must be open to and searching for His wisdom, always looking to Him for better ways of producing and marketing.

Here are a few other tips for making a profit based on my own experience:

SELL RETAIL

If you want to make a profit farming, especially today, then you need to focus on selling retail. Today the average farmer receives less than 12 cents (gross) of every retail dollar spent on food, as opposed to 40 cents in 1950. The rest goes primarily to food processors and distributors. When you are getting started in farming and are small-scale, it's very hard to make money selling wholesale because of the quantity required. Because of government subsidies, there are times wholesale prices are even below the cost of production. Therefore, the easiest way to get a return for your products is to sell them retail, as directly to the customer as possible. That way you get the other 88% of the dollar.

PRODUCE FIRST FOR YOURSELF

Another good way I have found to be profitable is by producing food and fiber for my own needs. (You can't get any closer to the customer than that!) Because the products don't change hands, there are no mark-ups and no taxes owed.

Let's do a theoretical comparison between buying $1,000 worth of vegetables, or growing them ourselves. This isn't perfectly accurate, but it helps illustrate my point. First we have to take into account that we will have to earn approximately $1,400 in order to have $1,000 after taxes. If we factor in that farmers normally receive twelve percent of every retail dollar spent on food, it leaves us with $120 for production, without deducting what the farmer charged for profit. This percentage holds true for home-gardeners as well. A recent article documented how one gardener grew $700 worth of produce on 100 square feet for less than $65. I believe we could safely say that for less than $120 you could grow vegetables that would have cost you $1,400 to buy. Also, you don't have to drive anywhere to get it. It just comes from the field to the table. You may not have exactly the economy of scale that the growers that sell at the store do, but most of the time what you produce is going to be superior in quality.

Most farmers today grow very little of anything they eat. They sell at low wholesale prices and buy at high retail. Therefore, it takes a lot more money for them to be able to make a living. If we want to decrease the amount of money our farms must make to provide a living, then we should be producing as much as we can for ourselves.

"REAL" COST OF $1000-WORTH OF VEGETABLES

PURCHASED FROM STORE	$1400
GROWN BY YOU	LESS THAN $120

LESS CAPITAL-INTENSIVE AND MORE LABOR-INTENSIVE

We cut costs and increase profit by setting up our farm to be less capital-intensive and more labor-intensive. This is especially helpful when you are starting out and don't have any extra revenue to invest in the business. Of course, I'm not implying that we should always do things the hard way or reject any tools that decrease labor. However, we must realize that on a small farm, costs can sometimes be kept low by doing things by hand instead of by investing in expensive machinery that isn't really justifiable. When you buy expensive tools or machinery you have to increase production in order to justify and pay for the machine. This results in a constant pressure to always get bigger. Many times you could just spend a couple of days, get the whole family together and do the job by hand, and make more profit than if you had bought a piece of equipment and shortened the time spent by a few hours.

Here are examples of jobs that can be done quickly with many hands: transplanting seedlings, harvesting potatoes, packaging eggs, etc. Rather than purchasing expensive equipment, get the family together and get to work. Sometimes it makes sense to rent a tool or a piece of equipment to help complete a task, or we can borrow equipment from a neighbor for a short time. Over time our hard work will allow us to invest in better tools that allow us to maximize human labor on the farm, but our goal is not to totally eliminate the work of our hands.

MULTIPLE CUSTOMERS AND PRODUCTS

Another tip for having an economically viable farm is to always have multiple customers and products, reducing the risk of losing all your market at once. It can be tempting at times to sell to one wholesale market, but that's not always the most secure or profitable strategy. It may make short-term sense, profit-wise, but in the long run it can break all your eggs because you have them in one basket. For example, if I can't make it to the farmer's market, I have other restaurants and stores to which I can sell.

Multiple products means more sales to each customer and less chance of your production completely failing. Capitalize on the marketing that you have already done. If you have a set of customers buying eggs from you and you begin producing strawberries and beef, some of those same customers will probably buy some strawberries and beef. When the coyotes kill your chickens, you still have your strawberries and beef to sell.

HOW CAN YOUNG MEN GET STARTED IN FARMING?

Because there are so few young farmers, there is a big need today for young men to become farmers. The problem is, most of them don't have the luxury of parents or grandparents who farm who can help them get started. Instead, their family is probably more likely to say, "Why in the world would you want to be a farmer?" I believe that God desires young Christian men to come and work the land and care for it. Therefore I have a few words of encouragement and tips for young men who desire to farm.

DON'T JUDGE YOUR SUCCESS ACCORDING TO WORLDLY STANDARDS

Many people will tell you how to be successful in life. They will judge you when you don't meet their standards. However, what you need to be concerned about is meeting the standards of success that the Lord has given you. Some people may think that you are wasting your life if you decide to be a farmer. If you are seeking the Lord and are farming for His Glory, then you will be successful according to His definition. Farming is a very honorable and rewarding profession. Consider how many people continue to farm even when they lose money! It's a calling that fulfills in a very fundamental way the desire God gave each of us to be fruitful.

MAKE SURE YOUR MOTIVES ARE RIGHT

If you are a Christian young man who wants to farm, you need to make sure that you look at your heart and make sure your motives for farming are right. Do you want to farm just because you think it will make you happy, or do you want to farm because of a desire to glorify and serve the Lord? If you don't build on the right foundation with the right heart, then you will end up being unsuccessful and unhappy.

SOW IN SEASON *(develop your skills)*

To be able to begin building a farm as a young man, you need to make sure that you sow in season. Proverbs 20:4 says:

> A sluggard does not plow in season; so at harvest time he looks but finds nothing.

When you are young you need to be preparing to be a useful man whom the Lord can use. If you sense that the Lord is calling you to farming, begin preparing as early as you can with what God has given you. Use every opportunity you have to learn the skills and knowledge you will need in farming. Read and ask lots of questions, then hold the answers up to Scripture. You will probably never have as much time as you do now to learn things. Sow in the season that you are in now, so when the time comes you can be prepared and equipped to be a Godly farmer.

Be Faithful in Little

If you want to farm, don't wait until you have more land, more tools, more everything. Be faithful with what God has given you right now. If your family lives in town and you have a small yard, then begin to learn how to care for it and grow things. If you someday want to have livestock, are you doing a good job taking care of the family dog? How can you expect the Lord to entrust you with more of His creation if you haven't done a good job with what you already have? If you can't be faithful with a window box or pet, then you probably won't be faithful with a garden or a farm. Start today! Grow something. Do a good job to the glory of God.

Seek Godly Farmers to Work with and Learn From

It's very hard to learn farming apart from doing it. One of the best ways to learn how to farm is by working with a godly farmer. Even if you only have access to a somewhat moral farmer, there are many things you can learn from him. Make sure that you filter anything you learn through God's Word, even things you learn from a godly farmer. Many older farmers I have met and talked to have excellent knowledge and wisdom in caring for the land and working with their hands, but they have a hard time finding help. Few people seem to appreciate their wisdom.

When I was preparing to farm I worked for several farmers without pay in return for the opportunity to ask questions and learn from them. If you are going to learn from someone, I suggest you don't work for pay unless you absolutely need the money. To justify paying you they will have to put you to work doing some unskilled job and you won't learn as much as you would if you were able to work alongside them and take time to learn things.

Be Very Humble

You and I know very little about farming. I believe the best farmer in the world has only begun to scratch the surface of all that there is to know about producing things from the soil. Don't ever be afraid to ask questions. Don't be resistant to rebuke or correction. If you want to become a wise farmer, you will listen. The more you know about farming, the more you will begin to understand how much you don't know. You can always learn more. Listen to someone explain something even when you think you already know it, because they will probably say something that you don't know. "Do you know what the brix level of a plant means?" they may ask you in the midst of a conversation. You may have learned a little about it before and want to say, "Yeah, sure!" However, I have found it to be much more helpful to respond with something like, "I have read or heard about it before, but could you explain it to me again?" If you want to be a wise farmer, you must learn to be humble.

BE WILLING TO START OUT AT THE BOTTOM

Farms take a lot of energy and work. Most of the time one won't be handed to you or placed in your lap. You will have to work for it and gradually build from the ground up. Starting a farm is often a multi-generational project and you need to be willing to be a stepping stone for future generations. I like to think that a lot of the work I am doing building our farm, improving the soil, establishing markets, creating infrastructure, planting trees—it's all a legacy for my children. They can move on beyond what I have done and build on my shoulders. That means I must be willing to to provide a foundation for them.

BE CREATIVE

As a young farmer you may not have many resources. Maybe you have family that can help you or maybe you don't. Don't be discouraged. God will always provide a way for us to do what He has called us to. If He has called you to be a farmer, then He will provide you the means to be able to do it. You just have to be faithful to use the resources He has given you in a creative way. Just because you don't own land doesn't mean you can't farm. You can rent land, or lease it. When starting out I would highly recommend *not* buying land so you can be flexible while learning and can better know what land you need. If you are limited in space there are lots of ways you can utilize small plots intensively. We usually have more resources than we think. We don't always have to go into debt. Look for creative solutions to your problems.

WHAT ARE SOME THOUGHTS ON MAKING THE TRANSITION TO BORN-AGAIN DIRT FARMING?

You may be saying, "I already have a farm. I am heavily invested in the way that I am currently farming. Some of the things you have said about farming to the Glory of God sound interesting, but as a practical matter I can't change the way I am farming right away!"

Let me encourage you by reminding you that born-again dirt is about changing our perspective and embracing the pursuit of God-glorifying agriculture. It is not about a particular method or practice. Most of us can't change our farms overnight. The farm is on the journey of sanctification along with the Christian farmer. We can change the direction of our farms today, but the result is a journey, not an event. The change will come as we pursue God's best for our farms.

We shouldn't view our farms as reformed, but as ever-reforming. They won't ever be "finished", so we need to simply focus on constantly evaluating everything we are doing according to the Word of God. We shouldn't get discouraged when we see how far we fall short. No matter what our farms are like now, the Lord is faithful and will provide us a way to bring glory to Him. Having born-again dirt means you have begun a journey of faithfulness in the little things, taking baby steps, one change at a time, moving towards God's glory.

HOW CAN WE PROMOTE AND SUPPORT BORN-AGAIN DIRT?

Here are a few practical action items for those of you who are interested in and passionate about God-glorifying agriculture, but don't have the opportunity to farm, except on a very small scale. Just because some of us aren't full-time farmers, it doesn't mean that our job of having born-again dirt is any less important.

1. SEEK TO BE BIBLICAL IN YOUR OWN VIEW AND APPLICATIONS OF AGRICULTURE

Even if you don't farm, you can promote born-again dirt by seeking to understand the Biblical principles relating to agriculture. Then try to find some way to begin applying some of these principles in your own circumstances. If possible, grow some of your own food. Begin to apply a biblical worldview to agriculture.

2. ENCOURAGE OTHER CHRISTIANS TO SEEK TO GLORIFY GOD THOUGH AGRICULTURE

Perhaps you know some Christians who are involved in agriculture. You can encourage them by communicating why and how we can glorify God though agriculture. Perhaps you could share this book with them. Share with other Christians about how agriculture is the foundational occupation of every economy, and if we, as Christians want to reform the economy, we need to start with agriculture.

3. SUPPORT GOD GLORIFYING-AGRICULTURE

Christian farmers won't be able to succeed by themselves. They need people like you in the Body of Christ to support them. Buy from and encourage farmers who glorify God in their care of the land, to the best of their ability. If we desire to see agriculture to bring Glory to God and we continue to support forms of agriculture that bring Him dishonor, aren't we being inconsistent?

CONCLUSION

I hope the Lord has used this imperfect book to encourage you as you seek to continue reforming your born-again dirt. I believe that Christians need to lead, not follow, in farming and food production. We can do that through humbly seeking to glorify God. Farming isn't monotonous, dull, manual labor fit only for the less capable people of society. Farming is challenging, fulfilling, satisfying work that honors

God and serves others. Let us strive to be faithful in the work God has given us. If we are faithful I believe we will be amazed at what the Lord can do through His people.

Imagine the impact born-again dirt could have on our nation. What if Christians began taking their job as stewards seriously, turning the country into a beautiful, fruitful landscape dotted with productive homes filled with godly families? What if Christians began to farm in a way that was sustainably fruitful, honoring the design of God's creation? What if Christians began to reach out and serve their communities by selling high-quality, healthy food? What if Christians began capitalizing on the lifestyle that farming offers, rather than just viewing the benefits of farming in terms of money? What if, when the world's systems of farming fail, born-again dirt farms continue to be vibrant and productive? I believe that the testimony of Christian farmers faithfully stewarding the land will provide us an opportunity to share the true source of our success—the Gospel of the Lord Jesus Christ.

May God grant us born-again dirt.

RESOURCES

THE BIBLE IS THE FOUNDATION FOR OUR FARMS, BUT GOD REVEALS WIS-dom to many people who have written helpful books. The following is a list of some that have been most helpful to me. I do not whole-heartedly recommend them all, but much useful information can be gleaned if Scripture is used as a filter.

GARDENING

Smith, Edward C. *The Vegetable Gardeners Bible.* North Adams: Storey Publishing, 2000.

One of my favorite books for backyard gardeners. Lots of great pictures and easy to understand.

Coleman, Elliot. *The New Organic Grower.* White River Junction: Chelsea Green, 1995.

Probably the number one gardening book I would recommend to market gardeners. Great advice on very high standards of production.

GETTING STARTED IN FARMING

Salatin, Joel. *Family Friendly Farming*. Swoope: Polyface, 2001.

> This book offers many practical tips and testimony regarding running a family farm.

Salatin, Joel. *You Can Farm*. Swoope: Polyface, 1998.

> This is the classic book that helped me grasp a vision for actually being able to farm for a living. Loads of practical advice regarding starting a farm, production, marketing, and much more. A must have for any farmer!

GOVERNMENT REGULATIONS AND IMPACT

Carson, Clarence B. *War on the Poor*. New Rochelle: Arlington House, 1969.

> This book is rather old, published in the 1960s, but does a great job documenting the negative impacts of government subsidies and programs on farming. Also covers the effect of Government interference in others areas of the economy.

Salatin, Joel. *Everything I Want to Do is Illegal*. Swoope: Polyface, 2007.

> A helpful book for understanding some about government regulations and how they effect farmers, and what farmers can do about it.

LIVESTOCK

Salatin, Joel. *Pastured Poultry Profits*. Swoope: Polyface, 1999.

> If you are interested in a small, affordable, yet potentially lucrative farm enterprise to start, then raising pastured poultry might

be a good thing to consider. This book covers the topic in detail, and is chock full of useful info from production to marketing.

Salatin, Joel. *Salad Bar Beef.* Swoope: Polyface, 1995.

This is a good book that describes a rotational model of grazing for raising grass-fed beef cattle.

Ussery, Harvey. *The Small-Scale Poultry Flock.* White River Junction, VT: 2011.

The author of this book has done much homestead research on natural raising of chickens on a backyard scale, including ways to grow your own chicken feed!

MARKETING

Lee, Andy, and Patricia Foreman. *Backyard Market Gardening.* Buena Vista: Good Earth Publications.

This is one of the best books I know of for information and advice about retail vegetable marketing. I have spent many hours in the winter reading this book while making marketing plans for the next season. It also has some good growing tips as well.

NATURAL DESIGN PRINCIPLES

Hemenway, Toby. *Gaia's Garden.* White River Junction: Chelsea Green, 2009.

I dislike the title of this book, but the information it contains gives such an awesome testimony of the brilliance of God's design and the benefits of using it that I still recommend it. However, be careful to filter what is said with Scripture. With my personal copy I used a marker to change the title to say "God's Garden"!

Mollison, Bill, and Reny Mia Slay. *Introduction to Permaculture*. Berkeley: Ten Speed Press, 1995.

This is a great book that focuses on farm design based upon natural patterns. It has great pictures and is easy to read. Written by non-Christians who nonetheless recognize the wisdom in God's creation.

MISCELLANEOUS

Cobleigh, Rolfe. *Handy Farm Devices and How to Make Them*. New York: Orange Judd, 1910.

I can spend hours pouring over this little book. It contains many ideas for making useful farm devices, with lots of pictures and diagrams. The quotes scattered throughout the book are also quite interesting.

WEBSITES

www.foundationsforfarming.org

An amazing ministry in Africa that is raising farmers' yields by applying scriptural and natural principles.

www.farming-gods-way.org

The old website of Foundations for Farming. Still has many useful resources.

www.thedeliberateagrarian.blogspot.com

A blog of Christian agrarian writings. Offers some quality home-manufactured tools.

www.redeemingthedirt.com

> The author's blog written for the encouragement of other Christian farmers.

www.truefoodsolutions.com

> An online community of Christians interested in food, homesteading, gardening, nutrition, farming, and more!

www.careofcreation.net

> A website concerning biblical stewardship of the land.

EXTRA MATERIAL

THOUGHTS ON TECHNOLOGY

The proper use of technology is quite an interesting topic, especially among Christian farmers who want to move away from the pagan worship of modern technology. I don't claim to know all the answers regarding appropriate technology, but since technology and tools are an important part of farming production, I will venture to make a few observations.

First, technology is a wonderful gift from God and is very helpful to us in the work He has given us. Man's development of technology is a way that we can reflect the image of God. God gave us the ability to create tools that allow us to do more work than we could without them. Physics and science are our servants to help us in the work of ruling creation.

Second, I believe that proper technology should seek to leverage the efficiency and marvelous design of natural biological technology, not replace it. It's often more effective to use the technology that God has made available to us in nature than to come up with our own technology to replace it, such as feeding grass to horses vs. trying to grow and process our own bio-fuel for a depreciating tractor. The technology in creation is astounding! Consider all the chemistry that has to happen in order for a chicken to eat a handful of grain and turn it into an egg and a days worth of work scratching and pecking. Think of the amazing fermentation process that allows cows to turn grass into something useful, like milk! When we need to accomplish something, it would be wise to ask if there is some biological creature that could do it, rather than buy the latest and greatest piece of equipment. Joel Salatin uses pigs to turn compost instead of purchasing a $50,000 mechanical compost turner, not only honoring God's wisdom and design, but making business sense as well.

Third, technology isn't spiritually neutral. If it's not developed to do the work God has given us, in a way God intended, then it's distracting at best and destructive at worst. When deciding to use a particular "time" saving technology or tool, we need to make sure that we count the costs. If a new piece of equipment increases our production at the expense of quality, then we should question whether it's going to help us or hurt us. The goal of farming is not to accomplish the most amount of work with the least amount of effort. The goal of farming is to glorify the Lord, and all technologies need to be evaluated on the basis of helping us or hindering us, as we accomplish that goal.

THE BLESSING OF WEEDS

I believe that even the consequences of the curse show's God's mercy. Just as the Lord uses pain and difficulty for our own good and sanctification, He also has provided good uses even for the thorns and weeds. Many plants that have thorns are useful: roses, blackberries, raspberries, even some fruit trees have thorns. Some thorny plants can also be very useful as hedges to protect yards and gardens from wild animals, or to keep people away from dangerous places. Briar patches and thorny shrubs provide protection from predators for rabbits and birds, something that was unnecessary before death entered the world through sin. Even many thistles and "weeds" have practical uses. The fluffy seeds and tough fibers of some thistles are useful, and some have herbal properties. It's hard to find a weed that is entirely noxious and useless altogether if managed properly.

Many weeds provide healing to the land that has been laid bare by man and would erode away. Here in Alabama, and much of the South, Asian Kudzu vine has taken over large areas of land and is considered a nuisance. However, much of this land is so poor and farmed out that Kudzu has few competitors. In our mature woods I have found old Kudzu vines that grew alongside and complemented the existing forest without taking over. In poor soil Kudzu controls erosion, fixes nitrogen, grows edible tubers and leaves, and produces sweet smelling flowers. Even in the "curse" of the Kudzu weed, our southern soil is being blessed by the merciful, healing hand of the Lord.

APPENDIX C

THE DANGERS OF CHRISTIAN AGRICULTURE

I AM A VERY PASSIONATE PROMOTER OF CHRISTIAN AGRICULTURE. I love farming. I believe that it is something God calls His people to (in a general sense, not every individual) and that it provides the opportunity for an integrated lifestyle of worship, work, family, and ministry. This is part of the message of this book, and since writing it I have talked to many, many Christians who are beginning to care for and work the land to some degree or another. I am very excited about the work the Lord is doing in the hearts of His people to give them a desire for taking back creation stewardship for His glory.

Recently, however, the Lord has begun to show me some of the dangers and traps associated with Christian agriculture. As with almost anything in life, we can so easily take things that are good and run with them until we take our eyes off of Christ and fall off the straight path. So I want to briefly share a few dangers I think we should guard against as born-again farmers:

1. PRIDE IN LIVING A "SUPERIOR CHRISTIAN LIFE"

Farming does not automatically make us better Christians. Indeed, there are many benefits to the lifestyle of agriculture that can help facilitate Christ-centered living, but farming itself is not some higher

Christian calling that takes us to the next level spiritually. I have even heard of stories where, when not done prudently, returning to the land and homesteading has torn families apart. Farming is something that we must do because that is what God has called us to, not because we think it will fix all our problems and make us happy. Because I love farming and am passionate about sharing the glories and benefits of it (even comparing it with other occupations), I have to guard against causing other brothers and sisters in Christ to feel inferior because they don't farm. "May I never boast except in the cross of our Lord Jesus Christ, through which the world has been crucified to me, and I to the world" (Galatians 6:14).

2. TRUST IN SELF AND SELF-SUFFICIENCY

One of the attractions of farming is that it allows us to work for "ourselves" and have more control over what we do and how we spend our time. It also allows us to produce a lot of what we need for ourselves (in terms of food and fuel) and be less dependent on buying things from others. However, while we are enjoying trying to be a have a more sustainable and self-sufficient farm we can easily fall into the trap of individualism, selfishness, and isolationism. And sometimes, while we may not be doing it as individuals, we may be guilty of doing it as a family. We need to realize that one of the main goals of our pursuit of sustainability and individual/family agrarian productiveness is not so we don't have to rely on others, but rather so that we can be in a position to help "carry each other's burden's" as God calls us to. God has created us to need one another in the body of Christ. Thus, while it is a good thing to seek to be independent of unbelievers and ungodly systems we must realize that we as Christian believers and families are intended to function together as the body of Christ, needing each other in order to be effective. "The eye cannot say to the hand, 'I don't need you!' And the head cannot say to the feet, 'I don't need you!'" (1 Corinthians 12:21).

3. Legalism and Trust in Methods

As born-again, Christian farmers, *how we farm* is important because we should recognize that we are accountable to God for how we care for his creation. But we need to guard against becoming too caught up in attaching the name of Christ to any particular method. To be sure, we need to be purposeful that the methods and practices we use honor the Lord, but that doesn't mean they are the only, or even the best, way for every farm to bring Him glory. If I have found that a particular gardening method is very fruitful and easy, and seems to honor God's design in creation, then I can share it with others, but I shouldn't start telling people, "If you are a Christian, then this is the gardening method you should use if you want God to bless you." We must beware of developing formulas and falling into legalism where we attribute our farming "righteousness" to a particular set of practices. It is God and God alone who blesses our farms and produces fruit. The way we farm should flow forth from a love for God and a passion to subject everything we do to the authority of Christ. And I don't think this would result in every born-again farm looking and operating exactly the same way.

4. Becoming a Workaholic

Farming involves a lot of work, as many of us know. If we want God to bless us as farmers we must be diligent in our work. There are animals to feed, weeds to cultivate, barns to build, customers to serve, crops to pick, fences to repair . . . and the list goes on and on. Work is a gift from God and can bring much satisfaction and fulfillment. But farm work, although demanding, is not the only thing God calls us to in life. There are wives to love, children to raise, neighbors to help, messages to write, hospitality to show, fellowship to enjoy, and souls to win. The beauty of farming is that many of these things can be integrated into the life and work of the farm. But I find that they can easily suffer from it as well. I have to remind myself on occasion that my success is not rated by what I can physically achieve in a given day. Let us guard against becoming Christian farm-aholics, and make sure we focus on sowing into the relationships in our lives as well as in our fields.

5. Considering "Simple living" as a Means to Holiness

Many Christians move to the country and take up farming/home-steading because they want to get away from the fast-paced, busy life of the city. The simple life of the farm can help many of us focus on what is really important in life by removing many of the distractions of the modern age. Some of us may even dabble with "off-grid" living. But a danger I would caution us against here is falling into the trap of viewing simple living as a means to holiness. Although there are benefits to being free from some of the luxuries and conveniences of the world, they do not equal righteousness. We are not automatically more honoring to God just because we grow a garden, cut our own firewood, or milk our own cow. Honoring God starts with the heart and those things are merely fruit. Are not many pagans doing those same things today? However, they are often doing it to feel better about themselves, not to honor God.

6. Judging other Farmers we consider "Worldly"

It is very easy, especially as we become more passionate about trying to honor the Lord in the way that we farm, to look down upon what we would consider "worldly" Christian farmers. Many of us have studied, prayed, and been convicted about the way that we farm, but we can subsequently begin to think that anyone who doesn't farm like we do must not really love Jesus. While it is fine and good to discuss the Biblical merits of this or that farming method, we must be very careful to judge the hearts of other farmers using our own standards. Only God knows the hearts of men. And at whatever point we judge another, we are guilty. Do you farm organically and think that industrial farmers are greedy? Well, since no one on earth is perfect, they probably are. But that same greed lies in your heart too, no matter how you farm. The Christian life is a journey of sanctification. None of us have arrived at a place where we perfectly honor God in our farming. We all have growing and learning and repenting to do. We need to show grace to one another, holding firmly to the truth while guarding against looking down upon brothers or sisters in Christ just because they are on a different part of the journey. Our goal should be to share our testimony of where God has brought us and what he has shown us and encourage each other in the right direction, which is Jesus Christ.

7. WORSHIP OF FARMING

As with many things in life I can easily allow farming to become an idol in my heart. Because it is such a major part of my daily life and object of my energies, it can quickly consume more of my heart than it should. I love farming! But woe to me if I should allow my care for the land to become my focus rather than my commitment to Christ! Agriculture should not be the center of my life, Christ should. Do I feel more of a bond with a fellow farmer than I do with a fellow follower of Jesus? Am I more willing to stand up for good farming stewardship than for the Gospel of Christ? That should give me a clue as to where my heart really lies. And cause me to fear. May I seek first the Kingdom of God. We as Christians should be some of the most passionate farmers in the world. Not because we just really, really love to get our hands dirty. But because we fiercely love the Savior of our souls and Creator of the world and farm wholeheartedly for Him.

SYNOPSIS OF BOOK

6　PRINCIPLES OF GOD'S DESIGN
What principles should direct our farming methods? **59**

11 GETTING STARTED: TIPS AND SUGGESTIONS
How can we start or support Born-Again Dirt? **143**

APPENDIX A
Resources **159**

APPENDIX B
Extra material. **165**

ABOUT THE AUTHOR

NOAH SANDERS lives with his wife and son near extended family in central Alabama where he manages a born-again dirt farm. Currently he oversees the production of chickens, eggs, vegetables, honey, milk, and fruit that go to feed his family and community. In addition to farming with his family, Noah enjoys playing the fiddle, reading, sketching, and blacksmithing. He also enjoys taking advantage of opportunities to provide encouragement to other young men regarding vision and biblical manhood.

To purchase more copies of this book, please visit
www.bornagaindirt.com!

COLOPHON

Display text set in Ed Merritt's Nevis;
book text set in 11-point ITC Baskerville Regular & Italic.

Typeset in Adobe InDesign CS5.5.

Made in the USA
Middletown, DE
29 March 2019